TEILHARD DE CHARDIN
ON THE EUCHARIST

Teilhard de Chardin on the Eucharist

Envisioning the Body of Christ

Louis M. Savary

Paulist Press
New York / Mahwah, NJ

Cover image by Igor Zh / Shutterstock.com
Cover and book design by Lynn Else

Library of Congress Cataloging-in-Publication Data
Names: Savary, Louis M., author.
Title: Teilhard de Chardin on the Eucharist : envisioning the body of Christ / Louis M. Savary.
Description: New York/Mahwah, NJ : Paulist Press, 2021. | Includes bibliographical references and index. | Summary: "Reinterprets and re-envisions traditional Eucharistic theology and related prayer forms to fit an evolving universe, and introduces some of Teilhard's evolutionary perspectives, showing how the Eucharist is a living symbol of the ongoing incarnation—or transubstantiation—of the entire cosmos"— Provided by publisher.
Identifiers: LCCN 2020023217 (print) | LCCN 2020023218 (ebook) | ISBN 9780809154920 (paperback) | ISBN 9781587688881 (ebook)
Subjects: LCSH: Lord's Supper—Catholic Church. | Teilhard de Chardin, Pierre.
Classification: LCC BX2215.3 .S28 2021 (print) | LCC BX2215.3 (ebook) | DDC 234/.163—dc23
LC record available at https://lccn.loc.gov/2020023217
LC ebook record available at https://lccn.loc.gov/2020023218

ISBN 978-0-8091-5492-0 (paperback)
ISBN 978-1-58768-888-1 (e-book)

Published by Paulist Press
997 Macarthur Boulevard
Mahwah, New Jersey 07430
www.paulistpress.com

Printed and bound in the
United States of America

Contents

Preface

IN THE DAYS when Catholics fasted from midnight before receiving
Communion and were convinced that the odds were quite slim that
Protestants would go to heaven, my mother had great admiration
for a Lutheran friend of hers. Mom told me, "The Lutherans don't
receive Communion every week, but when they do, Maxine spends
her Saturday preparing for it. I think she may be even more serious
than we are about it."[1]

Another story:

At Mass one day during communion time, a little girl was watching the rather glum and grumpy faces of some people as they returned
to their pews after receiving holy communion. The little girl whispered
to her mother, "Didn't the priest tell us that God was wonderful and
bigger than anybody?"

"Yes, dear. That's right."

The little girl whispered again a question to her mother: "And
didn't he say that when we receive communion, God comes to live
inside us?"

"Yes," the mother nodded.

"Well," asked the little girl with a puzzled look on her face,
"shouldn't God show through?"

Wouldn't it be nice if that little girl could look at people coming
back from communion and see God showing through on their faces?

I confess that I often find it difficult at a Sunday liturgy to experience the incredible reality of the Eucharist. There are a few moments
right after the consecration, as the priest holds high the host and the
chalice, when I can be totally present to the sacrament. For the rest of
the liturgy, I admit to being distracted by babies crying, restless children, people sneezing and coughing, certain people and the clothing
they wear. Even when I am walking toward the altar in the communion

line, I am focused on keeping my place, watching the person in front of me.

I remember to smile at the eucharistic minister handing the host to me—after all, the Eucharist is a banquet, a time of joy. But immediately I must decide whether the line to the sacred cup is too long and, if I add myself to the line, will I block the flow of other communicants? Up till now, I haven't given any thought to the body of Christ that lies on my tongue. I keep moving.

On my way back, I look to see if I can identify the pew where I had been sitting before communion. Entering the pew, I jostle my way past others who skipped the cup and are already in their places. I move to make room for others who brush past me. Finally, kneeling in my place, I can begin to reflect upon the divine event that has just taken place in my very being.

If many people in the pews like me have been distracted from eucharistic contemplation, I suspect that the priest celebrating the liturgy at the altar must deal with even more distractions. He must manage the entire liturgy. A moment after he receives the sacred host and cup, he must shift into action and organize a major operation, the distribution of communion to the entire congregation.

Perhaps, while handing the sacred bread to each person, he enjoys a split second of contemplation, picturing the host filling each person with divine grace as they put it in their mouths. But, as soon as the communion line ends, the priest has the busy task of cleaning and drying the various patens, ciboria, and chalices. A quick glance at his watch reminds him to hurry up because another liturgy will be starting shortly. He gives a final blessing, then joins the procession to the back of the church, where he must stop and greet parishioners gathered around him with requests and announcements.

Sadly, the priest celebrating Mass has more distractions to deal with than any layperson. He has hardly any time to reflect upon the great event he has just conducted and the miracle that has happened in his body and soul.

Fortunately for our congregation, in addition to daily Masses, the Blessed Sacrament is exposed for adoration in the side chapel, weekdays from 8:00 a.m. till 8:00 p.m. There, the faithful can come to spend undistracted time in the divine presence. Adoration time is when others like me get to savor the tremendous gift of the Eucharist.

Preface

Personally, adoration offers the time to slowly turn over in my mind all the eucharistic insights that the Jesuit priest Pierre Teilhard de Chardin shared in his writings. There in that chapel is where this book had its beginning and becoming.

I have been studying the writings of Teilhard (as everyone calls him) for over forty years. He was the first person to integrate the findings of modern science and evolution with Christian theology. He did it over a century ago. I was blessed to have discovered his evolutionary perspective soon after his writings were published in English. Only recently have people in the larger church community began to realize what a great contribution he has made to our knowledge of the workings of God.

I have immersed myself in Teilhard's ideas. Over many decades his vision has been slowly evolving in my own thought. So, whenever I write or lecture on Teilhard, I try to convey what I think he might be saying to us *if he were alive today*. His basic insights and principles remain as powerful as ever. What has evolved are the ways his wisdom needs to be presented to contemporary people.

My Purpose

Only near the end of the twentieth century did Christian theologians feel free to begin to rethink the story of creation in evolutionary terms. Teilhard did it at the *beginning* of the twentieth century. At that time, for a Christian theologian to reinterpret divine creation in evolutionary terms was a dangerous undertaking, especially in a church that had read the first chapter of Genesis *literally* for millennia.

More importantly, no one in the church took seriously the monumental challenge to *integrate evolution into Christian theology*—until Teilhard. He was the first to put together evolution and Christian theology into a coherent whole. Theologians doing it today are all standing on his shoulders. Awareness of evolution has invaded our daily experience. Words like *evolving* and *evolutionary* have become familiar words in business and in ordinary conversation. Words like *newness, transformation, innovation*, and *breakthrough* pervade our ways of thinking. Evolution changes our understanding of everything because it permeates every dimension of the universe.[2]

ix

Teilhard de Chardin on the Eucharist

In Teilhard's scientific treatise, *The Human Phenomenon*, he demonstrated that evolution was not merely a major force in the biological world but was the underlying and defining force operating at all levels of existence, animate and inanimate.[3] Teilhard was trying to show the church how evolution was important to God, especially to a God whose name is Love. After all, if evolution governed the development of the planets and stars—and everything else—from the very beginning, God had to be the one who invented the process of evolution in the first place. God had to be the one who established the laws that govern it. Since evolution impacts everything, Teilhard believed that it had to be integrated as an essential element of theology, spirituality, and moral life.[4]

The special question posed in this book is this: *How does Teilhard see evolution influencing our understanding of the Eucharist?*

Teilhard was not interested in theological or metaphysical debates about how the Eucharist is transformed on the altar or what transubstantiation means. Teilhard was a man of simple faith. He believed with all his heart and mind that the Eucharist is truly and actually the body and blood, soul and divinity of the living Jesus Christ. The Eucharist was central to his prayer life. Evolution enriched his devotion to it based on his evolutionary perspective of the body of Christ.

When he looked at the Eucharist in terms of evolution, he discovered that it shed much light on the richness and depths of God and God's work in the world. Much of the new insights regarding the Eucharist that he discovered arose through his prayer.

A cautionary note: If you are searching for traditional devotions to the Eucharist, this is not the book you want. Teilhard is far from traditional. He presents what may seem to some as a wholly original approach to the Eucharist. Teilhard's fresh exploration of the Eucharist has opened my mind and heart in ways I never imagined. I hope this book helps you to have similar experiences. His insights into the Eucharist will reveal to you much about the nature of God and the divine project God is currently accomplishing on Earth.

Regarding the book's structure, the first half is more theological and foundational. It explains Teilhard's key ideas about God, Christ, the Eucharist, Earth, people, science, and evolution. The second half takes many of these ideas and, from them, develops spiritual practices focused on the Eucharist. The first half of the book is designed to make you think, the second half invites you to pray.

Acknowledgments

SPECIAL THANKS to my Jesuit advisers and Teilhardian guides: Roger Haight, SJ, Robert L. Faricy, SJ, and Christopher Mooney, SJ. Thanks to Teilhard scholar Sr. Kathleen Duffy, SSJ, for her gentle and genial encouragement. Susan Timchak provided many wonderful suggestions to make my sentences clearer and more readable, as she has done for many of my books. William Lowry found ways to improve the text and caught typos everyone else had missed.

I am especially grateful to our pastor, Fr. Bill Swengros, of St. Paul Church in Tampa for introducing daily eucharistic adoration in our chapel. A daily period spent before the Blessed Sacrament has energized my spiritual life and generated many insights for this book.

I have long-standing gratitude for the pioneering commitment of HarperCollins for being the first to publish Teilhard's writings in the United States, beginning shortly after his death, and for keeping his works in print for many years.

I am grateful to Paulist Press for being willing to publish so many of my books on Teilhard. Donna Crilly and the Paulist editorial team have been most supportive.

For decades, my wife, Patricia Berne, has provided the perfect milieu of love and patience in which I live and write.

I
THEORY

Introduction
An Evolutionary Eucharist

FOR TEILHARD, the Eucharist provides a major link of continuity between Jesus of Nazareth and the Cosmic Christ. The Eucharist establishes an unbreakable connection between the small body of believers in the first century, the great body of believers on the planet today, and the throngs with whom Christ will rejoice when God's universal plan has been completed. Each day on our altars, Christ's eucharistic presence serves as a visible, tangible manifestation and guarantee of eternal life. It creates an organic bond of unity among believers in all lands, throughout all time, and into eternity.

Celebrating the liturgy today ties us to all those who celebrated the Eucharist, day after day in chapel, church, and cathedral, for the past twenty–one centuries. Sharing the same eternal covenant in the body and blood of Christ Jesus, we also remain connected to those who will be celebrating the Eucharist many centuries from now, perhaps even on other planets. The Eucharist assures a continuous divine physical presence among us until God's project is accomplished and the universe is united with God in an eternal loving union. The Eucharist also provides a way we continue to be nourished in faith and fellowship.

The Life of the People of God

The Eucharist is central to just about everything in the life of the church—its theology, liturgy, spirituality, sacraments, popular devotions, and daily life.

For many Christian denominations, the Eucharist is the heart of the liturgy. On the altar at every celebration, the Eucharist offers to God the Father a perfect sacrifice, not of blood, but of praise and thanksgiving. *Eucharistia* is the Greek word for "thanksgiving." The true meaning of sacrifice is to designate something as sacred or as a holy offering to God. A sacrificial offering does not require the shedding of blood.

At the eucharistic liturgy, gifts of bread and wine offered for consecration are carried to the altar by members of the community. After they are consecrated, the altar of offering becomes a banquet table for holy communion. From this table the faithful are nourished with Christ's very being. For many believers, reception of the Eucharist is the high point of their spiritual life. For daily communicants, the Eucharist marks a peak moment of each day.

For Catholic Christians, the Eucharist is also the epitome of the sacramental system. Among the seven sacraments, the Eucharist ranks highest. Reception of the Eucharist provides the culminating moment following reception of each of the other six sacraments. Eucharist is received after adult baptism, after confirmation, after reconciliation, after marriage, after priestly ordination, and after anointing of the sick.

In each Catholic church building, a burning candle quietly announces that the Eucharist is a living presence nearby in a sanctuary tabernacle. If one were to look down on Earth from the sky and could see every burning sanctuary candle in every church and chapel, the flames would cover the planet with a glowing blanket of divine light.

Some churches offer eucharistic adoration at certain hours during the day or night. In this devotion, the Eucharist is displayed in a monstrance on the altar so that people may look directly upon the consecrated host in silent, prayerful reflection. For those who can sense it, the entire chapel of adoration is saturated with the divine presence.

Popular devotions and prayers to Christ in the Eucharist abound in prayer books, pamphlets, and holy cards.

Historically, the eucharistic presence of Christ has been a topic of concern in theology.[1] Exploring the eucharistic mystery enriches our understanding of Christ, the Trinity, liturgy, the sacraments, and the church itself. Much of the church's source of energy and faith flows from Christ's real presence in the Eucharist. The holy bread and cup provide the spiritual nourishment that strengthens our faith and gives us the courage to act, even in the face of martyrdom.

The Eucharist has remained a central fixture of the church's liturgical traditions from its beginnings in the earliest Christian communities. In 1 Corinthians 11, St. Paul provided a description of the eucharistic liturgy as it was often celebrated in Christian homes and meeting places in the first century. In this letter, Paul provided the earliest scriptural record of the Last Supper event, at which Jesus first consecrated bread and wine.[2]

Teilhard's understanding of the Eucharist embraces all of this history, liturgy, and spirituality—and offers even more.

Teilhard's Perspective on the Eucharist

What Teilhard brings to our understanding of the Eucharist is an evolutionary perspective. He asks theological questions about Christ's presence in the Eucharist that have never been truly explored from an evolutionary perspective. For example,

- *Has evolution affected the eucharistic Christ? And if so,*
- *Who is the Christ present in the Eucharist today?*

The Catechism of the Catholic Church says that the Eucharist is "the body and blood, soul and divinity of Jesus Christ."[3] If we were to ask people to draw a picture of the person that emerges from that abstract doctrine—"body and blood, soul and divinity"—whose "body" would we see? The infant Jesus in the Christmas stable? The twelve–year–old Jesus in the temple? The thirty–year–old Jesus walking the dusty roads of Galilee? Jesus at the Last Supper? Jesus suffering on the cross? The resurrected Jesus on Easter morning? The risen Lord who seems to be able to take on various bodily forms, like that of a gardener talking to Mary Magdalene, or a fellow traveler walking on the road to Emmaus? Would we see the body of Christ that St. Paul describes, containing all believers as members or cells in that body? Does the Eucharist include all of these, or perhaps something even more?

Teilhard wonders, "How does evolution affect the Eucharist?" And, just as importantly, "How does the Eucharist affect human evolution's progress?"

What Does It Mean to "Evolve"?

Evolution is a confusing term to many, yet it has a simple meaning. It means *creating—or giving birth to—something new from something that already exists*. To describe the "something new," we say that the "something that already exists" has *evolved*.

An "evolved something" may be recognized as "something new" by the fact that (1) it still maintains its former essential properties and (2) it also possesses new properties or abilities that it never had before. Old abilities remain. New ones appear and are incorporated. The new properties that were never there before confirm the fact that an evolutionary step has been attained. These new abilities are called "emergent properties."

Most often, evolution happens when "parents" of two different species join to produce an offspring that possesses new and different qualities or abilities. Biologists call this mating of two different species *symbiosis*. However, evolution by symbiosis can happen on any level of existence—chemical, biological, emotional, intellectual, technological, or spiritual.

A common example of *chemical evolution* is (parent 1) *sodium*, an abrasive metal, joining with (parent 2) *chlorine*, a poisonous gas. The offspring of this unlikely symbiotic union is familiar *table salt*, which possesses distinctive emergent properties—the ability to season food, to help heal wounds, to preserve meat and fish. Neither sodium nor chlorine possesses any of the new properties of table salt.

Homo sapiens offers a good example of *biological evolution*. Human development may be traced back to the great apes that belonged to the primate phylum called *Homo*. The *Homo* genus branched out into the hominids, a category we humans share with the Neanderthals among others.

The telephone offers a good example of *technological evolution*. The telephone has undergone a number of evolutionary steps, from the landline phone to the cell phone. Few young people are aware that in the early days every telephone had to be attached by a cord to an outlet on the wall. Our great–grandparents' phones didn't go anywhere! They were stationary. The phone also evolved in its dialing abilities from a rotary dial to touch-tone buttons. The touch-tone phone, an evolutionary step, could perform new tasks that the rotary phone couldn't. For example, the touch-tone allowed commands—even ten–digit dialing—to be made with a single touch. In its many evolutionary stages, the landline phone evolved into the mobile phone, the mobile phone into the cell phone, and the cell phone into the multipurpose instrument of information, entertainment, digital storage, camera, and video recording so prominent today. In pockets and purses, phones today travel everywhere as "constant companions" to their owners. Through all its many evolutions and acquisition of new abilities, today's phone remains recognizable as a phone—a way of talking to people at a distance. None of the primary functions of the original telephone have been lost. Evolution has simply added many more.

Mathematics provides a recognizable example of *intellectual evolution*. Math has evolved from arithmetic and plane geometry into algebra, calculus, number theory, probability, statistics, matrix theory, stochastic processes, quantum computing, and a host of other mathematical specialties. Yet it is still mathematics. In all these evolved specialties, none of the abilities or functions of arithmetic or geometry has been lost. Only new abilities have emerged. Clearly evolution at work.

Each of us experiences *personal evolution* as we grow from infancy to adulthood. At each stage of growth, we acquire new attributes and abilities that we did not have at a previous stage. These emergent properties express their evolutionary appearance, over time, in our physical capacities, our emotional expression, our intellectual competence, our social skills, and our spiritual growth. *When someone evolves, none of the abilities or capacities essential to being a human person is lost or destroyed.* What changes in evolution is that new abilities and capacities are added.

Notice that evolution does not do away with what went before. *Evolution is not revolution.* Revolution gets rid of what went before. Evolution doesn't get rid of abilities previously developed or acquired; it keeps using them. More accurately, it enhances and transforms them. Jesus's Sermon on the Mount provides an excellent example of Jesus as an evolutionary teacher in *moral evolution*.

Jesus Evolves the Ten Commandments

In Jesus's Sermon on the Mount, he is explicitly evolutionary, not revolutionary. He assures the people that he has not come to destroy Jewish morality but to fulfill it. That's a good definition of evolution—

not to destroy but to fulfill. Jesus takes each of the Ten Commandments and evolves it.

- The commandment "Thou shall not [physically] kill" evolves into "Thou shall not mentally kill either," or even wish others dead in anger or revenge.
- The commandment "Thou shall not bear false witness" evolves into "Always speak the truth." No need to swear an oath; a simple yes or no or a handshake will do.
- Don't hate your enemy, but show him understanding and love.
- If someone needs a coat, give him your coat and other clothes that he may need. If someone slaps you on the cheek, don't punch him back; turn the other cheek. And so on.
- Go the extra mile to show kindness and compassion to everyone, whether you know them or not, whether you like them or not.

Notice that none of the *intentions* behind Jewish morality in the commandments are violated. In evolving each commandment, Jesus adds new types of behavior and motivation that weren't there before. The Ten Commandments are not done away with. Rather, their fuller potential is revealed. Jesus evolves them to find their deeper meaning and purpose.

The purpose of the commandments is not merely to serve as a guide for helping families and neighbors live together peacefully or for achieving social justice in the community. With Jesus, the Ten Commandments have evolved into *a process for creating a community of love and compassion*. As re-envisioned, the commandments are designed to eventually prepare everyone to experience the fullness of life (salvation).[4]

The Eucharist and Evolution

For Teilhard, evolution is not merely a theory or a hypothesis, but the most universal process happening on Earth—and throughout the universe. "Evolution is a general condition, to which all theories, all

Introduction

hypotheses, all systems must submit and satisfy from now on in order to be conceivable and true."⁵ Evolution is not merely a major force of biological life, it is also the underlying and defining force operating at all levels of being and life.⁶ It is the dynamic energy that drives everything forward.

In light of the pervasiveness of evolution, Teilhard would ask, *Is Christ evolving? Is the Eucharist evolving?* The Letter to the Hebrews states clearly, "Jesus Christ is the same yesterday and today and forever" (Heb 13:8). How then can Christ remain the same, yet be evolving?

Notice that Teilhard is not asking, Has the *theology* of Christ and the *theology* of the Eucharist evolved? Of course they have. Talk to anyone who has studied theology of the liturgy, the sacraments, church doctrine, and church history. For example, in the early church, the Eucharist was referred to as the Mystical Body of Christ, while the assembled faithful were called the "real" Body of Christ. In other words, for the early Christians, Christ was present in the consecrated bread and wine in a mystical way, or as a sacred mystery. It was less mysterious for them to envision Christ really and truly present in the community of believers. The members of the assembly saw themselves physically and spiritually as members of the real Christ Body. Paul states unequivocally, "Now you are the body of Christ and individually members of it" (1 Cor 12:27; see Eph 4:1–16).

Somewhere in a past century, people began doubting the divine presence in the Eucharist. They suggested that the consecrated host was little more than a symbol of Christ's living body. To combat this trend, theologians promoted a labeling flip. They began calling the consecrated host the "*real* presence of Christ," and referring to the assembled faithful as "the Mystical Body of Christ." The church as the Body of Christ, including all the faithful on Earth and in heaven, began to be described as a "mystical" entity, while the Eucharist was depicted as "real."⁷ For example, the lyrics of the fourteenth–century hymn *Ave verum corpus* ("Hail to the real body") clearly refers to the eucharistic host.

No one denies that, over the centuries, theological ideas regarding Christ and the Eucharist have evolved and deepened in understanding, perception, imagery, and application. Teilhard is not talking about doctrine evolving, but about *the living Christ himself evolving.*

Notice the final phrase in the *Catechism's* statement about the Eucharist:

9

In the most blessed sacrament of the Eucharist the body and blood, together with the soul and divinity, of our Lord Jesus Christ and, therefore, *the whole Christ is truly, really, and substantially contained*. (no. 1374)

Has the Mystical Body of Christ—"the whole Christ," which is Christ plus all the faithful who live in Christ—been growing, maturing, and developing throughout the centuries so that we can say that the "whole Christ" has evolved and continues to evolve?

Understanding "Collective" Evolution

Everything in the universe that is a product of evolution was born from something that went before it. The cell phone didn't just appear from nowhere. It was born from the generations of earlier forms of the telephone that went before it. In mathematics, the calculus did not just occur to some mathematician. It was born as a "child" in the minds of mathematicians familiar with its "parents"—arithmetic, algebra, and geometry—that came before it.

Not only can evolution be observed in individuals of a species, evolution also happens in the species as a *collective* entity. The human species possesses more capacities and abilities than the Neanderthals. Some of these advances include physical prowess, intellectual facility, emotional subtlety, social skills, artistic abilities, musical talents, spiritual endowments, and mathematical aptitude. They are the "emergent properties" of the human community, not just of one individual.

For example, the human community as a whole—*Homo sapiens*—has also evolved in the way it self–organizes, the way it forms relationships, groups, organizations, cities, states, and nations. Other collective evolutionary capacities include advances in science, technology, transportation, communication, knowledge storage, energy, government, health care, sanitation, urban planning, nutrition, and a host of other fields. Collective evolution is happening in all these fields. It encompasses much more than the quiet biological or neurological evolution that has been happening in our species over the past one hundred thousand years.[8]

The Eucharistic Question

Teilhard gives a name to the reality that is "Christ who is at one with all who live in Christ." Teilhard calls this immense Christ reality the "Universal Christ" or the "Cosmic Christ."[9]

Though theologians in Teilhard's day commonly referred to the body of believers as the Mystical Body of Christ, Teilhard seldom used that term. He preferred "Universal Christ" or "Cosmic Christ," because he saw the whole Christ as much larger and more inclusive than simply the members of the Roman Catholic Church. His Christ, like St. Paul's Christ, included all creation (Rom 8:22–24).

With the name *Cosmic Christ*, Teilhard can formulate more clearly his Christ question. His question becomes, *Is the Cosmic Christ evolving?*

This is an important question because the Cosmic Christ is the Christ that lives today—the *only* Christ that lives today. St. Paul tells the Christians in Corinth to focus on the Christ that lives today, not on Jesus of Nazareth. In a startling passage that we seldom refer to today, Paul writes,

> From now on, therefore, we regard no one from a human point of view [literally, "according to the flesh"]; *even though we once knew Christ from a human point of view, we know him no longer in that way.* So if anyone is in Christ, there is a new creation: everything old has passed away; see, everything has become new! (2 Cor 5:16–17, emphasis added)

Today, Jesus of Nazareth is no longer walking the roads of Galilee. Today, Jesus of Nazareth is no longer sitting at the Last Supper table. Today, Jesus of Nazareth is no longer hanging on the cross. Today, the Jesus of Nazareth in the crib and on the cross exists only in our memories. Today, two thousand years later, the Jesus Christ who lives and functions among us and through us is the Cosmic Christ.

More precisely, when we ask whether the Cosmic Christ is evolving, we are asking if the living Body of Christ on Earth—the believers as a loving community—have developed new skills and abilities and possess new competencies that enhance the Cosmic Body of Christ.

Does the Cosmic Christ today have more abilities than the Cosmic Christ had at an earlier period?

Jesus of Nazareth once predicted that we—those who had faith in him—would be able to do everything he could do and more. "Very truly, I tell you, the one who believes in me will also do the works that I do and, in fact, will do greater works than these, because I am going to the Father" (John 14:12). Has this prediction proven to be true?

Yes, indeed.

The most prominent abilities of Jesus of Nazareth were his abilities to heal illness and to cure people of mental or spiritual sickness (demonic possession). Jesus may have healed many people in one day. Today, we may not be able to heal by mere touch as Jesus did. Perhaps, sometime in the future, when human consciousness has evolved, some among us may develop this ability.

Nevertheless, today, hospitals around the world, many founded by believers, collectively heal tens of thousands of people every day. Technologies have helped develop surgical procedures and prosthetics that could never have been possible in Jesus's day, nor even a century ago. The Body of Christ on Earth evolves in its healing abilities each year as pharmaceutical laboratories develop drugs that help prevent and cure scores of physical and mental maladies. These companies have developed an arsenal of drugs to reduce pain and alleviate suffering. Today, biological science allows health-care technicians to adjust an individual's DNA by editing it, thus offering hope for a better, longer life for many. Medical technology is producing its own share of healings that would have been considered miracles a generation ago.

Our understanding of human consciousness and mental illness has also improved greatly in the past two centuries. Psychiatrists, clinical psychologists, therapists, social workers, and counselors have helped balance the emotional lives of many thousands of people suffering from mental illness, trauma, abuse, anxiety, and depression. Religious men and women in ministry have relieved people suffering from demonic torment.

This increase in physical and mental health evolves human society as a whole and thus affects the development of the Body of Christ. As examples of the healing of *social sickness*, most nations, originally founded on Christian principles, have enacted laws that protect against discrimination because of race, religion, disability, gender, age, and so on. Welfare laws have created sources of income, housing, food, and health care for the poor, sick, elderly, and disadvantaged. These are just some of the ways that the Body of Christ on Earth is evolving so that its members increasingly show care, mercy, and compassion to one another.

Improvements in travel and communication make it possible for people to build and maintain friendships and families no matter where they live, thus providing another advance on how members of the Body of Christ can express love and care for each other.

Organizations like Doctors without Borders, Habitat for Humanity, and thousands of other worldwide associations display love and compassion in ways that Jesus of Nazareth the man could never have imagined.[10] Opportunities to show love and build bonds of friendship abound in today's world. Believers have created orphanages, retirement communities, homes for unwed mothers, l'Arche communities for adults with disabilities. They have provided sanctuary places for immigrants, for captives of sex traffickers, victims of domestic abuse, refugees of war, and the homeless. Love abounds.

Of course, all around us hatred, greed, pride, selfishness, cruelty, and many other evils flourish, as newspapers and television broadcasts remind us daily. But where evil abounds, love abounds more (Rom 5:20). Millions of simple acts of love and care that happen in every community each day evoke little interest in news producers. But expressions of compassionate and creative love are happening everywhere. We have only to observe the goodness of people around us.

People of faith have created an immense educational system, from preschools to universities, making learning available to everyone. The internet, with sites such as Google and Wikipedia, enriched by the voluntary contributions of knowledge made by millions of anonymous people, provides a vibrant source of information and education, available in moments to anyone with a computer or cell phone.

Today's Body of Christ is healthier, more educated, more connected, more all–embracing than ever before. Today's Body of Christ possesses more resources, more abilities, more tools for improvement, more skills, more technology, and more ways to build connections and offer love than the Body of Christ one hundred years ago.

With each new advance — in technology, communication, transportation, health care, welfare laws for the marginalized, organizations that protect the abused and rejected, access to meaningful work, to education, to art and music, to new opportunities, to worship, to show compassion and mercy—the Body of Christ evolves. What the Cosmic Body cannot do today to foster loving union in the human race, it may be able to do tomorrow.

In this sense, Teilhard would assert that the Body of Christ on Earth and, therefore, the Cosmic Christ, is evolving. Teilhard might go so far as to say that "the whole Christ" is evolving daily, since some new advance in human development becomes available each day.

The question naturally arises, *Does the Eucharist evolve?* Teilhard might pose this eucharistic question by first asking, *Who is the Christ in the consecrated host on the altar today?* Does the Eucharist hold only Jesus of Nazareth as he was on Earth over two thousand years ago, sitting at the Passover table at the Last Supper? Or is it the Cosmic Christ who lives on Earth—in us and throughout the cosmos—today?[11]

If we can say that the Cosmic Christ is evolving day by day, can we say that the Christ in the Eucharist is new every day?

Teilhard's Unique Approach to the Eucharist

What is unique about Teilhard's approach to the Eucharist is that he begins by affirming that *God loves matter.* Matter is the tangible stuff of which our world and all of us are made—metals, minerals, liquids, salts, acids, enzymes, gasses, fungi, bacteria, and so on.

Teilhard points out an undeniable fact about God and matter. *God can reveal to humans who God is in the only way that God can— through matter.* God revealed God's divinity through matter in four major events:

> *First,* God revealed to us who God is by creating a magnificent evolving universe of matter.
>
> *Second,* in the fullness of time, God revealed to us who God is in the physical "matter" of Jesus of Nazareth's human body, born of a human woman.
>
> *Third,* God revealed to us who God is in the physical "matter" of the assembly of believers. Collectively, we are

the Body of Christ and, individually, members of it (1 Cor 12:27).

Fourth, God revealed to us who God is in the simple "matter" of bread and wine in the Eucharist at the Last Supper.

Sadly, for centuries our Christian churches have portrayed much of the material universe as unspiritual and dangerous. We were told that to believe in Christ meant leaving the material world behind. In church prayers, we were constantly reminded that the physical world is mired in sin, a place of exile, a valley of tears, and a den of temptations. We were taught to love God and hate the world. We were counseled to see Earth merely as a testing ground to determine our worthiness to enter heaven at death. We were instructed to desire only heaven. To do that, we were counseled to fight or flee the world of matter.

We were never taught that God loves matter.

Yet, it is so obvious. Since God created the universe out of love and the universe is full of matter, God must love matter. God keeps making the point that God loves matter. For instance, God loves to watch us create things out of matter and loves to see how the things we create out of matter grow, mature, and develop their capacities to reveal God to us. Look at scientific tools like microscopes that allow us to observe the nano world of bacteria and viruses in all its complexity. Or telescopes that track the moving magnificence of the galaxies. Or medical instruments and drugs that save our lives and enrich our health. Or technological inventions like cars and coffeemakers that make life easier and more enjoyable. All of them are nothing but matter.

God also reveals God's love of matter in each of the millions of new creatures in nature and among human beings that are born as flesh and blood on our planet each year. God chose to put the divine gift of an immortal soul into each person's living matter. This tells us not that God hates matter but that the Creator loves matter.

To keep his memory and his spirit alive, Jesus did not choose to feed us simply with spiritual inspiration and divine grace, but with the *matter* of his flesh and blood. When Jesus chose bread and wine to be the medium of communion with God and with each other, he exalted this simple form of inert matter. He chose it, not because God hated matter, but because God loved matter.

God continues to show us in a thousand different ways that matter is something sacred. The divine revelation expresses one powerful fact: living in matter means we are immersed in a cosmic–sized sacred reality. If the Eucharist reveals anything about God's nature, it tells us to love matter as much as God loves it. The Eucharist is the full revelation of God's "love affair" with matter.

For Teilhard, the best way to show love to God is by getting to know and love all the "matter" through which God shows love to us. This includes all nature on Earth and in the entire starry universe (see Col 1:19–20). Teilhard's mission on Earth might be summed up this way: to tell everyone that God loves matter, and the best way to find and fall in love with God is by falling in love with matter.

God loved material creation so much that God chose to give to it—especially to the planet of "matter" called Earth—the gift of his only Son *in the form of matter.* The incredible love that God has for the world that God created is the truth that Jesus was trying to tell Nicodemus. It is a truth that the church forgets again and again. Teilhard is simply reminding us of what Jesus told Nicodemus.

> For God so loved the world[12] [the cosmos made of matter] that he gave his only Son, so that everyone who believes in him may not perish but may have eternal life. Indeed, God did not send the Son into the world to condemn the world [the cosmos made of matter], but in order that the world might be saved[13] through him. (John 3:16–17)

Jesus, the Son of God, loved the world of matter as much as his Father did. Jesus loved matter so much that he chose to use matter to continually reveal himself to us in the Eucharist. At the Last Supper, he poured his very life into bread and wine, emptying himself into two forms of simple matter. He invites us in holy communion to enter into his divine life through matter.

Teilhard recognized clearly what God's love for matter implies. For Teilhard, it means that *all matter is eucharistic.* Matter, wherever we encounter it, continually invites us to enter into the life of the One who created it. Matter in all its forms continually reveals the Creator's love for us and matter's importance to us.

16

Introduction

Think of it. Matter is what enables us to be human. Without matter, we cannot communicate. Without matter, we cannot show love or receive love. Without the matter that forms our lips, tongue, and throat, we cannot speak. Without the matter of pen and ink, computer, or cell phone we cannot communicate at a distance. Without the matter of our bodies, we cannot laugh or cry, eat or drink, dance or sing, run or swim, blow a horn or doodle a cartoon, drive a car or peer into a microscope, wear colorful clothes or decorate a birthday cake.

Without matter, we cannot play a sport or cheer loudly for our favorite team. Without matter, we cannot enjoy a movie, plant a seed in the garden, curl up with a good book, or cuddle a kitten. We cannot attend an opera or jump and scream at a rock concert, look through old photos or cuddle a favorite coffee mug, watch a sunrise or enjoy a sunset. We cannot experience walking in the rain or catching snowflakes in the air.

Without matter, we cannot pray or worship together, light a candle, or bow in reverence.

Matter is always our teacher and guide. The resistance of matter challenges us to grow, adapt, invent, and evolve. Matter demands our attention and our respect. It encourages our hope and our determination. It accompanies us through success and failure. Matter forces us to learn ways to consider, compromise, compensate, console, and celebrate. Matter is always honest. It remains faithful to its materiality and its purpose. It never lies.

Your body is made up of atoms of matter. Each of these atoms in your body belongs either to you or to one of a thousand other bacterial species living in your organism. Every atom of matter is made up of subatomic particles. Each of these subatomic particles came into existence at the Big Bang. This means that every particle in your body is almost 14 billion years old. The elements in every atom in you are as old as the universe.

All the particles in the body of Jesus of Nazareth were as old as time. All the particles in every piece of communion bread and every drop of communion wine are elements of matter that are as old as time.

When you look at the host or the sacred chalice, you are looking at the risen Lord, who has made the entire evolving universe of matter a part of his body—in his cosmic body and in his eucharistic body. Perhaps the material universe has been his evolving body since the first moment of creation.

17

Teilhard de Chardin on the Eucharist

For Teilhard, discovering the multibillion–year evolutionary story of matter is central to understanding God's love for the cosmos and for humanity. Evolution offers a basis for a much richer appreciation of the Eucharist. It also offers a basis for a much richer understanding of Christian theology. Teilhard's insights about the Eucharist emerge from his basic principles about God's nature and the kingdom of God.

1

Some Basic Teilhardian Principles

God and the Kingdom of God:
A Perspective

BEFORE EXPLORING a fuller treatment of Teilhard's understanding of the Eucharist, some groundwork is essential in order to
see where his thought is coming from. He holds some basic principles
about God's nature and the kingdom of God that are not mainstream.
This chapter is provided for those to whom Teilhard's way of thinking
is relatively new.

If you are familiar with Teilhard's evolutionary and theological
principles, simply read over the list of principles below. If they are
familiar to you, you may skip to the next chapter. Otherwise, enjoy
delving into Teilhard's mind in the following pages.

Teilhard's Basic Theological Principles

BASIC 1. God is love.

BASIC 2. God loves matter.

BASIC 3. God put divine love into every particle of matter
at creation.

BASIC 4. God created an evolving universe.

BASIC 5. As God's love permeates matter, it naturally
generates a law of evolution within matter.

BASIC 6. The law of evolution eventually gives birth to life and eventually to consciousness.

BASIC 7. The law of evolution eventually gives birth to humanity.

BASIC 8. When humanity was ready to grasp God's purpose for creating the universe, God sent Jesus.

BASIC 9. Jesus presents God's evolutionary law of love as the way to bring "the kingdom of God" to its fulfillment.

BASIC 10. Within the kingdom of God, the law of love continues the evolution of matter toward spirit.

BASIC PRINCIPLE 1:

God Is Love

"God is love, and those who abide in love abide in God, and God abides in them" (1 John 4:16).

Although the church never denied that God was all–loving and all–forgiving, some teachers and preachers over the centuries chose to present God to the faithful as a strict judge. They often described the Creator as one who would as readily assign us to hell as welcome us into heaven. People were taught to see God more as a severe ruler than as an unconditional lover.[1] This focus led to centuries of preachers who promoted a fear–based spirituality and ethic.

Such anxiety–generating and guilt–ridden spirituality has remained a fixture in the church since the Middle Ages. Teilhard himself grew up immersed in it. In challenging it, he felt a need to explicitly affirm the primacy of the "God is love" principle. It serves as the basis for all the other principles.

Once we acknowledge that the very nature of God is love, it becomes obvious that God wants our love and enthusiasm for life much more than our anxiety and fear.[2] "There is no fear in love, but perfect love casts out fear; for fear has to do with punishment, and whoever fears has not reached perfection in love" (1 John 4:18).[3]

In the Gospels, Jesus reminds his disciples of the mutual love continually flowing between him and his heavenly Father, and of the divine loving Spirit that he and the Father share, which unites them

20

(John 14:15–21). During his final supper with his disciples, he leaves them with only one commandment, a love commandment, to "love one another as I have loved you."

In letters written by the apostle John to the Christian communities, the "God is love" theme occurs again and again. "God is love, and those who abide in love abide in God, and God abides in them."[4]

In his first letter to the people of Corinth, St. Paul offers a paean of love. While the virtues of faith and hope are very important, says Paul, they are nothing compared to love. Love stands out as the greatest virtue. Moreover, love is eternal. It will be the primary energy expressed forever in heaven with God (1 Cor 13:1–13). Love is what makes heaven *heavenly*.

Following the theology of John the Evangelist and St. Paul, Teilhard grounds his theological thinking on a definition of *God as Love*. God "created this universe out of love and for love."[5]

BASIC PRINCIPLE 2:
God Loves Matter

In the beginning, God spoke a creative Word and the universe was created. God saw that it was good (Gen 1:12, 18, 25, 31). Or, as John the Evangelist expressed it much more powerfully: "*God so loved the cosmos* that he gave his only Son" (John 3:16, altered).

What makes up this cosmos that God created? It began simply as a universe of matter. Nothing but lifeless matter. From what we have learned from science, the first moments of the universe appeared as a chaotic explosion of innumerable elementary particles of inert matter. From a single point, a universe full of protons, electrons, neutrons, and photons of light began expanding in all directions in empty space.

The creation of the universe was God's first act of self–revelation. Creating, wherever it happens, is typically a form of self–expression. Artists know this fact. God is an artist. "All creation—all matter—is the outpouring of God," says Richard Rohr. "What else could it be?"[6] The birth of the universe was God giving us the first self–disclosure of divine creativity and of the divine nature. We might say that creation was the first published Bible.[7] At the Big Bang, God was manifesting himself outside of himself, as it were, in a totally fragmented way. This explosion into existence of countless lifeless particles of matter was the first articulation of God's artistry. During eons of time, vast numbers of atoms connected to form billions of stars and planets. Billions of stars organized themselves to form billions of galaxies, yet all of them are nothing but formations of lifeless matter.

Planet Earth was formed out of lifeless matter about four billion years ago. At least one billion more years of transformations passed before Earth's matter gave birth to its very first forms of cellular life deep in the seas. This means that for at least eleven billion years since the Big Bang, God had been continually giving existence to a creation that was nothing but lifeless matter. Nevertheless, during those early eons of time this lifeless matter kept joining, connecting, unifying, and self–organizing. Even today, most of the universe is made up of lifeless unconscious matter—metals, minerals, liquids, and gases. We have learned how to work with all these forms of lifeless matter by joining, connecting, unifying, and organizing them.

Teilhard reminds us that John announced that the Word of God also loves matter, since the divine Word took part with God in this original creation. The Word "was in the beginning with God. All things came into being through him, and without him not one thing came into being" (John 1:2–3).

The divine Word of God also chose to be incarnated in matter. "And the Word became flesh and lived among us" (John 1:14).[8] He made his home with us here on Earth. A Divine Person entered matter and became a flesh–and–blood human being called Jesus of Nazareth. He had hair, teeth, toes, fingernails, wore clothing and sandals, got dirty and dusty, drank water, had an identifiable voice, lived in a family, attended synagogue, slept on a mat. He was immersed in matter, in his own body and all around him in people and things—baking ovens, wineskins, carpenter tools, sacred scrolls, furniture, shawls, urns, coins, writing tablets, thorns, bushes, grape vines, olive trees. All very tangible matter.

The bread and wine that Jesus chose to use for the great eucharistic sacrament are forms of inert matter. This communal sacrament involved eating and drinking, actions that only human bodies can perform. As C. S. Lewis wrote, "God never meant man to be a purely spiritual creature. That is why He uses material things like bread and wine to put new life into us. We may think this rather crude and unspiritual. God does not: He invented eating. He likes matter. He invented it."[9]

The obvious conclusion from this avalanche of evidence is that God loves matter, loves being immersed in matter, loves being involved in the workings of matter, and loves eating. Some of the greatest images of the heavenly kingdom were described as dining at wedding feasts.[10]

How are we to respond to these facts that show God's love of matter? St. John Damascene (675–753) explained how to honor matter without worshiping it: "I do not worship matter. I worship the God of matter, who became matter for my sake and deigned to inhabit matter, who worked out my salvation through matter. I will not cease from honoring that matter which works my salvation."[11] Many people are still waiting for the coming of God, unaware that God has already manifested the divinity in various ways at different times *in matter*, especially in Jesus of Nazareth and in the Eucharist. We can only anticipate with eagerness the many ways God will continue to manifest the divinity to us in the days and years ahead. For those with the eyes of faith, God in Christ continues to reveal himself anew to people thousands of times and ways each day during eucharistic liturgies all over the world under the appearance of matter, namely, bread and wine.

BASIC PRINCIPLE 3:
God Put Divine Love into Every Particle of Matter at Creation

Why does God love matter so powerfully? Because God put divine love and the spirit of love into every particle of matter in creation. Once we acknowledge that divine love—and divine spirit—permeate matter, it answers many very fundamental questions, such as the following:

- Why did the countless, individual original elementary particles at creation *not* remain separate and solitary?
- Why didn't these lifeless particles that made up the original universe simply keep randomly whirling about by themselves forever?
- What made them experience Attraction to each other to form Connections that became atoms?

- How did their connecting give various atoms different qualities, since hydrogen, helium, oxygen, carbon, sodium, chlorine, and each of the hundred or so elements in the table of chemical elements emerged, each possessing uniquely different properties?

Teilhard would answer each question like this: Because God is love. Creation must be an expression of God's love, for the divine can only express its own nature. Since God's nature is love, whatever God creates must be imbued with God's love. It is the very nature of love to join and bond with others, for love is intrinsically relational. For Teilhard, divinity united with the matter of the universe by permeating the universe of matter with God's love energy from the beginning.

Attraction and Connection are the most basic forms of energy—and the most basic forms of *love*. Attraction and Connection are the only ways by which inert particles can show "love." God put into each inert particle the drive to attract and join together. For Teilhard, the divine spirit of love drove the elementary elements to unite and form atoms, molecules, stars, and planets.[12]

Love becomes a cosmic force. Love wants to relate, to form connections and unions. Love creates the drive in things to continue to evolve by connecting and forming new unions or units. This attractive and bonding energy has been operating in creation since the first moment of space–time. There is no reason to think that love has exhausted itself or that it has run out of energy. On the contrary, love looks forward to creating more love, deeper love, more transforming love. Love looks toward the horizon and anticipates what awaits there.

Teilhard recognized that "love is the most universal, the most tremendous and the most mysterious of the cosmic forces."[13] God is the divine, transcendent source of love that energizes evolution, "that draws an entire universe, and not just human history, toward an unfathomable fulfillment yet to be realized."[14] No other quality or energy beside love would be able to account for the evolutionary nature of God's creation or its purpose.

For Teilhard, God who is infinite love "penetrates everything."[15] Love saturates the universe.

BASIC PRINCIPLE 4:
God Created an Evolving Universe

We who live in the twenty–first century find it hard to imagine that just a few centuries ago most people held what is called a "static" or "fixed" view of the universe. It is a very ancient and strongly held belief, but it also is an unwarranted assumption. It accounts for the description of the universe found in the early chapters of the Book of Genesis. According to Genesis, every species that exists today was individually created during the first six divine days (Gen 1:11, 21, 24–25). In the time of Jesus most people held a "static" understanding of creation. At that time the only changes people recognized were cyclic, such as the changing of the seasons and phases of the moon.

In the nineteenth century, an earthshaking discovery was made: *all living things are products of evolution.* Only after Charles Darwin published his book *On the Evolution of Species* (1849) did people begin to rethink the story of creation in evolutionary terms. Rethinking God's cosmic handiwork in evolutionary terms was a scary proposition, especially to the church and a faith tradition that had taken the first chapter of Genesis *literally* for millennia.[16]

At first, theologians simply dismissed the idea that evolution might have anything to do with theology. Some simply denied the evidence. Others argued logically, based on the premise that if evolution wasn't accounted for in Scripture, it could not be true or relevant. Others suggested that evolution was only an unproven theory, so it was unnecessary to deal with it. Psychologists might describe this situation among theologians as the church "in denial."

No one in the church took seriously *the monumental challenge to integrate evolution into theology*—until Teilhard. Early in the twentieth century, Teilhard the priest–scientist tried his best to get the official church to recognize the possibilities it was missing by denying evolution. He wrote,

> Evolution has in a few years invaded the whole field of our experience....This evolution is giving new value as material for our action, to the whole domain of existence...providing human aspirations (for the first time in the course of history) with an absolute direction and an absolute end.[17]

Evolution changes our understanding of everything because it permeates every dimension of creation.[18] Teilhard was trying to show the church how evolution was important to God. God was the one who created evolution and established the laws that govern it. Evolution, Teilhard believed, must become an essential element of theology.

Evolution is not merely a theory or a hypothesis, Teilhard insisted, but the most universal process happening on Earth—and throughout the universe. Teilhard was clear. He wrote, "Evolution is a general condition, to which all theories, all hypotheses, and all systems must submit and satisfy from now on in order to be conceivable and true."[19] Teilhard was showing that evolution was not merely a major force in the biological world but provided the underlying and defining force operating at all levels of existence and life.[20] For him, evolution impacted everything, even our theology, spirituality, and moral life. It is always driving the universe forward, seeking new fields to transform.

Traditional Christian theology, spirituality, and morality needed —and still needs—to undergo a kind of Copernican revolution in order to deal with the fact that God did not create a fixed and unchanging universe. Earth is not a cyclical and steady–state planet.

In Teilhard's terminology, he would say that the universe is not a finished cosmos but a *cosmogenesis*—a universe in process of becoming what it was meant to be. Planet Earth is a *geogenesis*—a planet in process of becoming what it was meant to be. The concept of genesis describes an ongoing, developmental process of birth and becoming that has a direction and a goal.

The universe has not yet reached its goal. It keeps moving forward stage by stage. Like any human child, the universe underwent a conception, a period of development, a time of birth. Like a growing child, the universe—and for us, planet Earth—is proceeding through its infancy, youth, adolescence, and adulthood.

Transformations and developments driven by evolution continue to happen on all levels of existence. Evolutionary changes are happening in communication, transportation, technology, media, commerce, farming, ecology, politics, medicine, mathematics, physics, chemistry, anthropology, psychology, and so on. Recognition of the breadth and depth of evolution has changed everything we thought we knew about ourselves and our purpose on Earth. For this reason, evolution has also affected theology, spirituality, and morality.[21]

Since life continues to evolve, evidence suggests that from the beginning God has had an evolutionary plan or project going on. We humans are called to play a role in that process. Jesus called this divine project the "kingdom of God." Jesus came to Earth to enlist our loving cooperation in the ongoing work of building the kingdom of God. Only in an evolutionary world would God need or wish for our personal involvement in furthering God's work on Earth.[22]

Since God the creative Creator made evolution so central to God's purpose, it is logical to say that God loves evolution. God loves to see people and things evolve. Teilhard would say that if God loves evolution, we should love it too. For Teilhard, simply to believe in God and serve God is no longer enough. "We now find that it is becoming not only possible but *imperative* literally to *love* evolution" (Teilhard's emphasis),[23] and to love in advance whatever it discovers.

When you love someone or something or some process, you want it to succeed and become all it can become. Christians are called to love evolution dynamically: "no longer merely to ease the suffering, to bind up the wounds, to succor the weakness, of mankind; but, through every form of effort and discovery, to urge the powers of love, right up to their higher term."[24] As they say about warfare, it is not enough simply to care for the wounded, it is important to achieve the objective.

In this light, Christians are called to approve and support evolution wherever it is occurring. If you can make evolution happen in some way, large or small, in some field or among some people, do it. As Teilhard puts it, "Love God in and through the universe in evolution." This is his constructive and all–embracing rule of moral action.[25]

BASIC PRINCIPLE 5:

As God's Love Permeates Matter, It Naturally Generates a Law of Evolution within Matter

Once we acknowledge the overwhelming evidence for evolution, Teilhard says, we must look for what drives and governs its movement. Can we recognize evolutionary patterns? Can we identify rules or laws that govern evolution? Can we track the path of evolution's advance? Can we glimpse where it may be leading us?

Much evolution going on in nature appears to be governed by seemingly random activity. Biologists point to natural selection, adaptation to environment, artificial selection, chance mutations, and other forms of gradual change. Many scientists see biological evolution as totally accidental, arbitrary, and unintended—perhaps even going nowhere in particular.

However, in sifting through facts in the multibillion–year history of the universe, Teilhard recognized (1) a *law of evolution* at work and (2) *evolution's direction.*

First, despite the apparent randomness and ups and downs of evolution, Teilhard noticed a consistent pattern. He recognized what appeared to be an underlying law governing evolution, one that could be more clearly observed over very long periods of time. He called it the law of "Complexity–Consciousness," a two–stage process. Over time, living species continued to grow more and more complex, both individually and collectively. At the same time Consciousness continued to expand and deepen—from sensation and perception to thought and self–reflection.

However, as we saw in principle 3, the evolutionary law has two earlier stages: Attraction and Connection (*union* in French). When combined, a more complete four–stage version of Teilhard's evolutionary law may be stated as the *law of Attraction–Connection–Complexity–Consciousness.*[26] Once you grasp the four stages of this evolutionary law, you realize how familiar it is to almost everyone.

In simplest terms, this is how the law of evolution plays out in all physical, biological, mental, and social domains. First, *Attraction leads to Connection.*[27] This is the familiar process we use to form friendships, families, partnerships, teams, communities and all other forms of interpersonal unions and Connections—all of which we trust will lead to a better life. We find ourselves attracted to someone or something—or someone finds us attractive—and we make a Connection.

All Connections and personal bonds begin with Attraction. Attraction is a most fundamental force in the universe.[28] It affects all levels of existence, from subatomic particles, to atoms, to molecules, to cells, to bacteria and all living forms of plants and animals. We humans are attracted to others and others are attracted to us because we are all made for union and communion.

In turn, *Connections lead to Complexity*. Whether we like it or not, Connections inevitably bring Complexity into our lives. Think, for example, of a newly married couple learning to live together. Or a person starting work at a new job at a large office. Or initiating a new friendship. Each new Connection or relationship forces us to deal with new personalities, new demands on our time, new responsibilities, and the relational conflicts and confusion that arise and call for broader understanding and forgiveness. We learn to make allowances and compromises to preserve the Connections we value. This is the experience of Complexity. We accept the challenges posed by Complexity because we trust they will lead to a better life for us and for others.

Finally, *Complexity leads to Consciousness*. To make sense of each new element of Complexity and to integrate it into our lives and loves, we must stretch our Consciousness to make it more all–embracing, more understanding. We no longer think merely of ourselves, our wishes, and our wants. Our hearts and minds must stretch beyond earlier self–focused boundaries to open to wider horizons. We begin considering the needs of others, of family members, friends, colleagues at work, neighbors, the unemployed, the needs of our city, our nation, and the world.

In summary, stages in the law of evolution that Teilhard clarified were *Attraction–Connection–Complexity–Consciousness*. That was his first discovery. His second discovery was that evolution was moving in a certain direction—*to higher and higher stages of Consciousness*.

BASIC PRINCIPLE 6:

The Law of Evolution Eventually Gives Birth to Life and Eventually to Consciousness

Since life continues to evolve, evidence suggests that God, from the beginning, has had an evolutionary plan or project going on. Now that we understand this evolutionary plan, we humans are called to play a role in that process. This divine process is moving in a certain direction; it has a purpose and a goal. It is God's great work. Its continued progress must become the focal point of theology, morality, and spirituality. It becomes what Teilhard scholar Ilia Delio calls the "power of attraction toward what lies ahead."

In his book *The Human Phenomenon*, Teilhard traces the law of Complexity–Consciousness from the Big Bang that initiated space–time almost 14 billion years ago. In its beginnings, the universe could be described as nothing but countless individual subatomic particles and photons of light. When looked at from that original chaotic starting point, the story of the universe's evolution is a chronicle of development from Connection to Complexity, from particles, to more complex atoms, to even more complex molecules, to even more complex compounds, to the stunning complexity of living cells, to the unbelievable complexity of plants and other living species.

The clearest way of characterizing evolutionary progress is to use to the measure Teilhard called *Complexity*. Scientists use numbers and counting to measure the variables of *distance* and *time*. Teilhard said it was time to use numbers to quantify the variable of *Complexity*. Why? Because *the universe's story may best be told as a narrative of continually increasing Complexity*. And, as is clear in the evolution of life forms, each stage of increasing Complexity demands a corresponding increase in Consciousness.[29]

What is important to recognize, Teilhard points out, is that *the law of evolution needs matter in order to operate. God needs matter in order to build the kingdom of God.* Without matter, Complexity could not grow, nor could spirit emerge. Teilhard writes,

> It is matter that gives the things of this world their radical capacity to enter into higher or lower synthesis, under one and the same Spirit. The essence of materiality would appear to be to make beings capable of unification. In this regard, there is no difference between [the process of unification] in the natural world and [the process of unification in] the new world that is being formed around Christ.[30]

St. Bonaventure (1221–74), an early Franciscan mystic, taught that "as a human being, Christ has something in common with all creatures. With the stone he shares existence; with plants he shares life; with animals he shares sensation; and with the angels he shares intelligence."[31]

BASIC PRINCIPLE 7:
The Law of Evolution Eventually Gives Birth to Humanity

As an experiment, Teilhard suggests that we imagine ourselves as modern–day observers who time travel back to different stages of cosmic evolution. For example, suppose you and I were present at the Big Bang and could see nothing but endless subatomic particles swirling around us. And suppose God were to say to us, "These little things are going to turn into stars, planets, moons and form billions of solar systems like your sun, planets, and moons."

We might respond, "No way!"

Continuing the experiment, suppose we were to time travel billions of years forward to the era on Earth when the big apes were about to branch out into various species of hominids, but all we could see around us were big apes. And suppose God were to say to us, "These fellows will soon evolve into species that discover fire, build homes, invent tools, learn to draw pictures, and begin to develop languages."

Unable to see beyond these hairy creatures grunting and swinging their arms, we might again say, "No way!" And yet it happened.

Now, transpose roles. Suppose you and I were to meet Teilhard himself a few weeks before his death in 1955. And imagine we were to say to him, "Less than fifteen years from now, Americans will be landing on the moon and we will watch it, live, on television. Then, within fifty or sixty years, humans will be carrying cellular phones with them wherever they go. With these cell phones that people keep in their pockets or purses, they will be able to connect almost instantly to anyone in the world. These phones will help guide people driving to any location on any continent. They will provide instant access to information that you can only get today from a library or a research journal. They will take photographs and save them or send them to other phones. Like a movie camera, they will capture and record live action happening nearby. On the screens of these phones, people will play games and compete with one another, watch movies, manage their bank accounts, and buy merchandise without going into a store. People will even be able to sell their own things on a worldwide virtual store. They will be able to download any of your published books—yes, your writings will be published—and read them as if they were holding a book in their hands. With these phones, they will be able to take photographs or make movies, and they will store all those photos and movies on that same phone and will be able to call them up instantly."

Teilhard might respond, "No way!" He never imagined it would happen so quickly. Yet here we are.

Teilhard predicted the appearance of a new global consciousness early in the twentieth century, but he never imagined it would happen so quickly.[32] The power and universal presence of a global mind has become more and more evident each year. The global mind, clearly revealed in our cell phones, is growing, developing, maturing.[33] In Teilhard's own words, "With every day that passes it becomes a little more impossible for us to act or think otherwise than collectively."[34] He died long before the internet was created, but he envisioned the globally unifying mental effect technology would have. Teilhard called the global mind the *noosphere*.

The noosphere (from the Greek *nous*, meaning "mind") is an evolving layer of thought and emotion that covers the entire planet, just as layers of water (*hydrosphere*), air (*atmosphere*), and life (*biosphere*) cover the entire planet.

The evolving global mind (noosphere) has enabled us—one might even say "forced us"—to become conscious daily of the concerns and needs of just about everyone on Earth. Our planetary mindset requires a morality and ethics designed to advance the consciousness of the human race.

As a species, we are moving from a national mentality ("America is the most powerful nation in the world") to a global mentality ("We need to care for the health of our planet"). We no longer see ourselves merely as separate nations but as one world, one people, one immense complex—and conscious—family.

Today, not only are individual lives intertwined, but also nations themselves. Nations are financially interdependent because the health of each major global financial market influences the health of all the others. Decisions of persons who get elected in one nation can influence other nations far away. Spiritually, people of many different religions are sprinkled throughout each country and, we can only hope that, instead of fearing and mistrusting each other, they are gradually learning to respect each other and learn from each other.

BASIC PRINCIPLE 8:

When Humanity Was Ready to Grasp God's Purpose for Creating the Universe, God Sent Jesus

Why else would the Word of God come to Earth to live among us and teach us unless God wanted to involve us *consciously* in helping complete God's grand project?

John says that Jesus Christ came as the light of the world. He came to enlighten us. "What has come into being in him was life, and the life was the light of all people. The light shines in the darkness, and the darkness did not overcome it" (John 1:3–5).[35] At the first moment of creation, "God joined in unity with the physical universe and became the light inside of every thing....Light is not so much what you directly see as that by which you see everything else."[36]

Guiding creation to the fullness of life is a divine project and that project is still in process. It has been evolving since the beginning of time. Jesus knows the Father's plan. He knows the Father's wish that the divine plan become manifest—be revealed. It is God's love project for creation. This project has a purpose and a goal. Jesus states this goal in his personal prayer, the Lord's Prayer, which he taught to his followers. "Thy will be done on Earth as it is in heaven." The goal is to turn life on Earth, as much as possible, into the love–filled life as it is lived in heaven.

BASIC PRINCIPLE 9:

Jesus Presents God's Evolutionary Law of Love as the Way to Bring "the Kingdom of God" to Its Fulfillment

Jesus proposed a radically new perspective on life and a new purpose for life. In this, he revealed his role as a prophet.

In his classic book *The Prophetic Imagination*, theologian Walter Brueggemann writes, "The task of prophetic ministry is to nurture, nourish, and evoke a consciousness and perception alternative to the consciousness and perception of the dominant culture around us."[37] Jesus prophetically offered an alternative consciousness.

When Jesus says, "Repent, for the kingdom of heaven has come near" (Matt 4:17), the word "repent" in Greek is *metanoia*. This Greek word does not mean to be sorry for one's sins. Rather, it means to put on a higher (*meta*) mindset (*noia*). It invites us to enter a higher or more inclusive way of thinking and seeing that serves as an "alternative to the consciousness of the dominant culture." Once we shift into this new *metanoia*, we may be able to see God's hand at work all around us.

Along with this shift in perception, Jesus proposed an alternative way to live. His "way" was designed to foster and nurture an evolutionary world created *by* love and *for* loving. His heavenly Father created the universe for a purpose. The Father had a plan for creation, and Jesus showed us how to cooperate in the fulfillment of that plan.

God's great evolutionary work on Earth and its continued progress—since it is far from complete—stand at the forefront of theology and spirituality. Evolution becomes what Teilhard scholar Ilia Delio calls the "power of attraction toward what lies ahead."

For Teilhard, this power of attraction toward what lies ahead is the way God primarily influences us humans in the evolutionary process.[38] Not only do we live in Christ and God at present, but God is also ahead of us in time beckoning us forward.

Every parent knows this experience of "being ahead" as it applies to their child. Parental love is both *in* the child, but also *ahead* of the child in time beckoning it forward. Think of the scene on the day their child takes its first steps alone. The child is standing by itself *knowing it is loved by the parent*. The parent moves a few feet in front (ahead) of the child and beckons it to walk forward toward the parent's open arms. The parent is inviting the child to take an important evolutionary step—to move forward on its own—into the parent's loving arms. Driven both by evolution and by "love ahead," the child takes its first faltering steps toward those loving arms. The child takes its steps because it knows that it is loved (within) and that the power of attraction (ahead) is the same loving force. It all happens within the energy of love.

BASIC PRINCIPLE 10:
Within the Kingdom of God, the Law of Love Continues the Evolution of Matter toward Spirit

For Teilhard, the way God works in our lives is by inviting us to take our next steps in growth. God's love is both in us and ahead of us. The future possibilities and potentials that we see in ourselves are not only inspirations of God within us but also invitations of God ahead of us. For Teilhard, this is how and why we explore, create, and expand our consciousness. Consciousness involves awareness plus appropriate action.

As our consciousness expands to include more and more people, it grows to be more and more like the loving, all–embracing consciousness of God. For this expansion of consciousness to become more and more all–embracing, it requires a *metanoia* process. *Metanoia*, putting on a new way of thinking and seeing, doesn't happen all at once.

Sadly, some people never experience this *metanoia* and may stay locked up in their personal lives and interests. Luckily, many others continue to develop wider and wider interests. Teilhard believes that humanity will reach a tipping point, when there are more people with expanding consciousness than those who are locked up.

It is important to recognize that today there are many who have evolved in consciousness and have already developed "a sense of the human." Think of the thousands who work with Doctors without Borders, the Heifer Project, Oxfam, the World Health Organization. These are people who see all humans as part of the human family, members of the world household who need to be fed, housed, educated, and cared for medically.

As Teilhard writes, "We are united to Christ by entering into communion with all people. We will be 'saved' [made whole] by an option that has chosen the whole."[39] We can hope that those who have chosen to enter consciousness of the whole will willingly embrace — and carry forward on their shoulders — those who are still locked up.

Here too, Teilhard acts as a prophet in that he is attempting "to nurture, nourish, and evoke a consciousness and perception alternative" to the current consciousness. He invites all people, not just believers in Christ, into a *metanoia*, a higher way of seeing things.

He wants more and more people to learn to "see" this *whole*. He is calling us to begin to develop what he calls "a sense of the human," the realization that our consciousness is meant to embrace everyone. As a human family in this century, we are indeed on the road to reaching "a sense of the human," but we still have a long way to go.[40]

These ten principles integrate Teilhard's thoughts on God, love, creation, evolution, matter, humanity, and consciousness. They provide a basic evolutionary theological framework from which to explore specific theological topics. In the following chapter, we apply Teilhard's theological principles to his understanding of the Eucharist.

2

Teilhard's Eucharistic Principles

Who Is Jesus Christ in the Eucharist?

T HE MATERIAL in this chapter underlies and supports all the subsequent material in this book. It presents ten basic Teilhardian principles regarding the Body of Jesus Christ and his eucharistic presence.

Although some of these principles are not commonly heard in church preaching, they are grounded in the writings of St. Paul and John the Evangelist as well as on those of the early fathers of the church. "Frequently in his theological writings, he [Teilhard] repeats that what he is doing is simply transposing into an evolutionary framework the great cosmic affirmations of St. John and St. Paul regarding the Person of Christ."[1]

Some Teilhardian Eucharistic Principles

EUCHARIST 1. Jesus Christ as the risen Lord remains both fully divine and fully human in the Body of Christ (the Ecclesia, or church) and in the Eucharist.

EUCHARIST 2. Jesus Christ announced the divine project, assumed charge of it, and instituted the Eucharist.

EUCHARIST 3. The Eucharist reveals that the body of believers, individually and collectively, are members of Christ's Body.

EUCHARIST 4. The Body of Christ, head and members, forms an inseparable organic whole.

37

EUCHARIST 5. Members of Christ's Body remain identifiably alive forever in his Body, even after they pass through physical death.

EUCHARIST 6. The risen Jesus Christ reveals that the evolving physical universe is his Body.

EUCHARIST 7. Jesus Christ as head of the Body, though divine, always retains his physicality.

EUCHARIST 8. The Body of Christ will continue to evolve until it achieves its total fullness at the end of time.

EUCHARIST 9. The Eucharist is a manifestation of the evolving Body of Christ and guarantees that the divine presence will remain among us until the divine project is complete.

EUCHARIST 10. The Eucharist builds unity in the Body of Christ and nourishes its members.

EUCHARISTIC PRINCIPLE 1:

Jesus Christ as the Risen Lord Remains Both Fully Divine and Fully Human in the Body of Christ and in the Eucharist

This first eucharistic principle merely restates perennial church teaching as found in the *Catechism* and professed in the Nicene Creed. The essentials of Jesus Christ today remain the same as they were in Jesus of Nazareth. Today, as then, he remains truly divine and truly human. Whether Christ is manifested as the risen Lord of creation or present in the Eucharist, it is truly the same Person, body and blood, soul and divinity.[2]

For Teilhard, Christ is always the Person of Jesus—Jesus transformed, but always in continuity with Jesus of Nazareth. The person who is head of the Cosmic Christ is the Person of Jesus, still in process to becoming all he can be in his Cosmic Body.[3]

Traditionally, it was believed that humans could add nothing to God, since God was perfect and complete in every possible way. God was almighty, all-knowing, all-seeing—total perfection. Moreover, everything that a perfect God created had to be perfect. In this traditional picture of creation, God could not create anything that was imperfect. Yet, as is quite evident, creation is far from perfect. The traditional view explains this apparent contradiction by asserting that humans marred God's perfect creation. It asserts that humans introduced sin into creation, eventually producing a world full of evil and suffering. Therefore, the most important reason that God's Son became human was to redeem us from our sins.

From an evolutionary perspective, Christ's purpose for living among us takes on a more positive role that includes, but goes beyond, redeeming us from sin. Jesus assured us of redemption from sin, but his mission involved much more than that. The Son of God came to Earth primarily *to establish the kingdom of God among us.* To accomplish this, he was all about transforming the human race on Earth through the power of love. Our task, then, is to reenvision our world as an *evolving* world. We see that God created a "perfectible" world. God wants us humans to continue improving and maturing in our ability to love one another.

Notice the difference. In the traditional viewpoint, God created a perfect world; humans ruined its perfection by sin. Jesus redeemed the world from sin by his death on the cross and made it perfect again. The problem with this viewpoint is that the world is still full of evil and sin. It is far from perfect.

An evolutionary perspective begins, not with a perfect universe but with a very "immature" universe. The universe was full of "evil" eons before humans emerged on Earth. Among its primordial evils are natural disasters, including hurricanes, tornadoes, floods, droughts, earthquakes, ice ages, and meteor strikes. Among animal species—evolved long before humans—other evils included sickness, physical handicaps, death, confusion, conflict, killing, pride, greed, gluttony, lust, and laziness. Humans today are still dealing with all the above "evils." This is evidence that the universe and our planet are still immature, still evolving, still perfectible. In this "perfectible" context, Jesus's ministry and mission of building the kingdom of God on Earth is full of possibilities for human activity.

Jesus announced this more positive and ongoing purpose for his coming to Earth in the beginning of his public ministry. "From that time Jesus began to proclaim, 'The kingdom of heaven has come near [or is at hand]'" (Matt 4:17). Jesus's many parables clearly show that revealing presence of the reign of God on Earth and moving this divine project forward are central to his mission.

His parables of the kingdom describe an organically developing and expanding transformational project. Parables of the sower and the seed emphasize the *organic* and *developing* nature of God's project as well as its *universality*; the mustard seed, its *expanding* nature; and the yeast leavening the dough, its inner *transformational* aspects. In Jesus's mind, the kingdom of God was and still is *in process*. Earth, including the human race, is still in the process of becoming what God meant it to be. Christ still has much work to do to accomplish his mission on Earth: "I came that they may have life, and have it abundantly" (John 10:10).

In Teilhard's language, just as Earth is undergoing the developmental process of *geogenesis*, it is also undergoing the process of *Christogenesis*.

Jesus Christ is the same forever, and Christ is still dynamically alive in his risen Body. We, who are the members of Christ's Body, are maturing and evolving *in* Christ. Teilhard would characterize this maturing process happening within the Cosmic Body of Christ by saying that humanity is evolving in complexity and consciousness. Given our current stage in the evolutionary process, the human race still has a long way to go before becoming fully mature. One might say that at present the human race is still in an early adolescent phase of maturing consciousness.

Evidence of humanity's current immaturity is incontrovertible. Just look at how often we are confused about our decisions, overconfident in our abilities, blind to our true potential, afraid to make commitments, impatient for results, and easily distracted. Our brains fixate on recent events and blow them all out of proportion. Obviously, we haven't yet evolved to our fullest potential.[4]

EUCHARISTIC PRINCIPLE 2:

Jesus Christ Announced the Divine Project, Assumed Charge of It, and Instituted the Eucharist

As its contribution to the divine project, humanity is called to continue evolving, expressing ever–higher forms of creativity and love. For us to experience the fullness of life is the goal of God's project. For

Christ to lead us on the way to the fullness of life (salvation), he had to become one of us. As Teilhard puts it, "If he is to be the soul of our souls, he must begin by being the flesh of our flesh."[5]

Christ came to us through a human woman, Mary of Nazareth. He was born in a stable in Bethlehem of Judah, he grew up "in age and grace" in Nazareth of Galilee. He was baptized in a baptism of *metanoia*[6] by John the Baptist in the River Jordan and began his public life in Capernaum near the Sea of Galilee. He gathered twelve apostles and began to announce the active presence of God's reign. He described God's plan in his Sermon on the Mount, his inaugural address. Through a life of creative, healing love he demonstrated how God's people were meant to live and treat others. He affirmed his divine appointment by healing the sick, driving out evil spirits, and revealing the nature of God. He explained to us that God is love — specifically, that God is a loving Father.

On the evening before his death on the cross, Jesus celebrated a sacred meal with his apostles and other disciples. There in the Upper Room, Jesus instituted the ceremony of his body and blood, and instructed his followers to reenact this ritual whenever they gathered to remember him.

On the very day of his resurrection, Luke tells us, the risen Lord himself reenacted the eucharistic ritual, when he stopped for supper on the road to Emmaus with two of his disciples. They recognized him in the breaking of the bread (Luke 24:30–35).

For Jesus, the Eucharist was the clearest way he could continue to fulfill his promise to remain physically present to his followers — within them and surrounding them — until the end of time. For his followers, the Eucharist reminded them that their true life was their life in Christ.

Whenever the apostles reenacted the eucharistic meal, they understood that the bread and wine became, in truth, his body and blood.[7] Jesus said, "This is my body" and "This is my blood." He did not say, "This bread is a symbol of my body" or "This bread is a substitute for my body." For them, it was his flesh and blood — his very life — that they were consuming and that would transform them.[8]

The Eucharist remains a mystery that is very difficult to grasp.[9] Despite the strength of their faith, early Christians found it easier to look at the assembly of believers gathered for Eucharist and see themselves as Christ's own body, than to see the bread and wine as the body and blood of Christ. For them, the Eucharist was primarily *the mystery*.

Today, in a reversal of perception, we readily affirm the Eucharist as "real," while we find it more difficult to see the people of God as the Body of Christ. Seeing ourselves living in the body of Christ is more mysterious to us. So, today we label the body of believers as the *Mystical* Body of Christ.

EUCHARISTIC PRINCIPLE 3:

The Eucharist Reveals That the Body of Believers, Individually and Collectively, Are Members of Christ's Body

St. Paul asserts this principle but states it in an indirect way. "Whoever, therefore, eats the bread or drinks the cup of the Lord in an unworthy manner will be answerable for the body and blood of the Lord" (1 Cor 11:27). Not only do such people mock Christ, says Paul, they also betray the believing community, which is the Body of Christ.

Paul reminds his Corinthian readers that as an assembly of believers they form the Body of Christ. "Now you are the body of Christ and individually members of it" (1 Cor 12:27). He explains to them how the Body of Christ operates. "For just as the body is one and has many members, and all the members of the body, though many, are one body, so it is with Christ. For in the one Spirit we were all baptized into one body—Jews or Greeks, slaves or free—and we were all made to drink of one Spirit" (1 Cor 12:12–13).[10]

When Paul uses the word *church*, or more precisely *Ecclesia* (Greek for "assembly"), he is referring, not to a worldwide hierarchical organization headquartered in Rome that we today sometimes call "the church," but to the body of believers gathered together in Christ who are participating in the Eucharist.

Early in his ministry, Paul seemed to identify the Body of Christ with each local believing community. Later, he began to realize that it was *all believing communities together* that formed the Body of Christ. All local churches lived in Christ as part of his body and all were longing for their fulfillment as one Body. In time, Paul further recognized that the Body of Christ had to be much more than just the believing

42

communities. He realized that all nature and all humanity had to be parts of Christ's Body, since all longed for their fulfillment (see Rom 8:19–25).

Teilhard goes even further. For him, the entire universe must be the Body of Christ, since Christ is "all in all" (see Col 1:15–20; 3:11). Richard Rohr put it very simply: "If you live within the cosmos, you live within Christ."[11] When Teilhard uses the expression *Body of Christ*, he sees the whole of creation—but especially humanity—as Christ's Body with Christ as its head, or "center." Jesus the Lord is the center of his Cosmic Body.

For Teilhard, a "center" means a point or place of convergence, the place that gives meaning to the whole.[12] "If the world is to be thinkable, it must be centered…by the Divinity himself who has introduced us *'in et cum mundo'* [in and with the world] into the triune heart of his immanence."[13] Christ serves as a personal center for humanity and the material world. Christ's head and his Body are inseparable. For Paul and Teilhard, the head, or center, of the Cosmic Body is a divinity whose name and nature is love.

If God is love, then the purpose and goal of God's project must be the active loving union of all creation. God's project, then, is clearly a *relational* project, ultimately a project of universal unity. It is all about building wider and more all–encompassing loving relationships on Earth.

Naturally, the aim of a project of an all–loving God requires continual growth in everyone's ability to love and to build loving relationships. This love in each of us is meant to become evermore all–embracing of others. In a Cosmic Christ that includes everyone and everything, there can be no exclusions and no competition. Christ's message calls for cooperation and collaboration among all people. There is no "us and them."

Teilhard came to realize that his evolutionary law, described earlier in basic principle 5, is in fact a law of love. The same four stages of the evolutionary law—Attraction–Connection–Complexity–Consciousness—also explain the way love operates. For him, love is the strongest, most universal, and most mysterious of the cosmic energies. Love begins with Attraction and leads to Connection. "The first essential is that the human units involved in the process shall draw closer together, not merely under the pressure of *external* forces, or solely by the performance of material acts, but directly, center to center, through *internal* attraction."[14]

Ilia Delio emphasizes the critical importance of this basic property of internal attraction: "Teilhard realized that if there were no internal propensity to unite, even at a rudimentary level—indeed in the molecule itself—it would be physically impossible for love to appear higher up, in a hominized form."[15] Teilhard describes these "forces of attraction between humans [to be] as powerful in their own way as nuclear energy appears to be."[16]

For Teilhard, although God loves every individual personally and unconditionally, the divine project calls for all of us to work together in loving teams to transform our world in love. Only loving group effort can bring all creatures and creation together into one great loving union. "That they may all be one" (John 17:21).

In contrast to traditional subjective and self–focused spirituality, Teilhard proposes an interpersonal and relationship–focused spirituality, which also demands new ways of looking at morality and ethics. God, who is love, must be intimately related to what goes on in creation. Otherwise, God would be less than pure love. God loves us, and God needs us to love God in return, to complete the relationship bond. For Teilhard, our lives and our work, individually and in teams, fill out God's relational self.[17]

It is important to notice a paradox inherent in loving. Achieving the fullness of being in union with others requires a kind of unavoidable suffering or emptying of self (*kenosis* in Greek). Spiritual writers call this process "becoming selfless." As the primary example of selflessness, the Word of God, who is the very fullness of life, empties himself in the incarnation by becoming a finite human being. Jesus showed us that God's unconditional love is also a self–emptying love.[18]

In the Eucharist, the Word of God, who is fullness of life, empties himself in a far more radical way than he did in becoming a human. He chose to express his fullness of life and love selflessly by being squeezed, as it were, into a wafer of bread and a small cup of wine. By emptying himself in becoming Eucharist, the lifeless matter of bread and wine becomes life-giving.

In Jesus of Nazareth and in the Eucharist, God models for members of his body how to empty oneself in order to truly love others, to become the servants of others, as he was.[19] This emptying of self may often require some form of suffering—or even dying—to manifest love for others. This is the meaning of Jesus's paradoxical statement: "Those who want to save their life will lose it, and those who lose their life for my sake will find it" (Matt 16:25). The one who refuses to empty oneself of self–concern and self–preservation in order to truly love another has already "lost his life."

Fortunately, there are many followers in the Body of Christ who are willing to empty themselves of their self–importance and entitlement in order to serve others and care for creation. In their helping to build the universal Body they will find the fullness of life (salvation).

For many, salvation represents a single event, namely, "getting to heaven." For St. Paul and for Teilhard, *salvation is a process by which one is gradually opened to the fullness of life.* The complete fullness of life may be experienced only in heaven in the direct presence of God. Nevertheless, people following Jesus's way may continue to experience life more and more fully. Someone has suggested that whenever we see the word *salvation* in a Scripture text, we might replace it with *the fullness of life.*

This is the paradox of the kingdom of God: self–emptying and abundance of life go together. This paradox is made manifest in the incarnation, suffering, death, and resurrection of Jesus: *the abundance of life is found through self–emptying*—sometimes to the point of suffering and death.

EUCHARISTIC PRINCIPLE 4:

The Body of Christ, Head and Members, Forms an Inseparable Organic Whole

The head of Christ's Body is the physical Person of Jesus of Nazareth risen from the dead. So, theologically speaking, *God's project may be described as bringing to fulfillment a Person,* whom Teilhard has called the Cosmic Christ. We live and move and have our being in that divine Person. We humans as a species are slowly maturing to perfect ripeness within this divine milieu called the Cosmic or Universal Christ. Our Head is leading us on this maturing journey of ascent toward divinity, the term of which Teilhard identifies as the Absolute.

The Absolute towards which we are ascending can wear only the face of the whole….It is not I that have laboriously discovered the whole; it is the whole that has presented itself to me….It is the attraction of the whole that has set everything in motion in me, has animated me, and given an organic form to everything.[20]

Teilhard gave a name to this organic process of creation's loving maturation in Christ. He called it *Christogenesis*. *Genesis* is a word that describes a process of birth and development. The first book of the bible is called Genesis because it describes the birth and development of the human race in its relationship to God.

Christogenesis reveals that Christ in his Cosmic Body is still in the process of becoming the mature universal "whole" he was meant to become. Christ has not yet reached his fullest potential, because the human family — part of his Body — is still developing, growing, maturing.

For St. Paul and Teilhard, Christ's Body is continually being perfected.

According to Paul, the Lord was equipping "the saints for the work of ministry, for building up the body of Christ, until all of us come to the unity of the faith and of the knowledge of the Son of God, to maturity, to the measure of the full stature of Christ" (Eph 4:12–13). Despite this glorious vision of the mature Body of Christ, Paul is quite aware of the immaturity of some of his new converts (see 1 Cor 3:1–9).

Bringing the whole divine Body to its fulfillment is God's project. For Christian believers, it is the most important project happening in the universe. Furthermore, it is an ongoing evolutionary project.

From this perspective, obeying the Ten Commandments becomes merely a small part of a much larger lifetime moral commitment to building the Earth toward the loving unity that God envisioned for it. Morally, instead of focusing on avoiding "sins of commission," Teilhard focuses much more on "sins of omission." Sins of omission are those activities that we could be doing (but are not doing) that would keep the evolutionary process moving forward and upward toward God's vision for us as a whole people.

Christ has not yet reached his fullest potential in us. For someone to reject the divinely created evolutionary process, so obviously at work in every area of life, would be to reject God's will. "Thy will be done on Earth."

But what is that divine will *for us in our day*?

For Teilhard, God's will for us *in our day* is to work at Christogenesis. He urges us to participate actively in this process. For him, it is morally imperative to try in every way to help bring about the maturation of the human family, to share in its searching, its hopes, its accomplishments.[21] In a very real sense, with God's help, we humans — especially in the decisions we make and the work we undertake — are mainly responsible for the future of humanity and the planet. "One may say that until the coming of Man, it was natural selection that set the course of morphogenesis and cerebration, but that after Man it is the power of [human] invention that begins to grasp the evolutionary reins."[22]

This change — placing the evolutionary reins in human hands — marks an evolution in spirituality that is much like the Copernican evolution in astronomy. Instead of a fixed and localized spirituality that revolves around the safety, security, and salvation of the self, it becomes a spirituality that refocuses on what each person, in cooperation with others, can do to foster what God is doing in transforming our world. In this new perspective, one's life purpose becomes so much larger and part of a much grander plan than one's own personal salvation. It includes the safety, security, and success of the whole divine project.[23]

When receiving holy communion, the priest or eucharistic minister places the sacred host in your hands and says, "The Body of Christ." These words are spoken so that you recognize that you are receiving Christ himself. But what is Christ himself saying to you in that precious moment, when he is a small host resting in the palm of your hand?

When Jesus Christ hung helplessly on the cross, he said to his God, "Father, into your hands I commend my spirit." When you are receiving holy communion, Jesus Christ, helplessly confined to the host, is saying to you, "My friend, into your hands I commend my Body." He is asking you to accept responsibility for what happens to his universal Body on Earth today in whatever ways you can help. Christ is entrusting to your care the many members of his great Body that you will meet today.

To you, Christ is entrusting the other believers who are celebrating the sacred liturgy with you. As Christ directly nourishes you with the grace and energy of his divine life, he is asking you to expand your attentive care to those around you. This is the kind of eucharistic prayer that Teilhard wants to explore with you.

47

EUCHARISTIC PRINCIPLE 5:

Members of Christ's Body Remain Identifiably Alive Forever in His Body, Even after They Pass through Physical Death

Teilhard's understanding of the Body of Christ describes "a love between God and creatures that preserves and accentuates their [individual] differences."[24] And, adds Paul, preserves them forever:

> Listen, I will tell you a mystery! We will not all die, but we will all be changed, in a moment, in the twinkling of an eye, at the last trumpet. For the trumpet will sound, and the dead will be raised imperishable, and we will be changed. For this perishable body must put on imperishability, and this mortal body must put on immortality. (1 Cor 15:51–53)

Thus, for Teilhard (and for St. John[25] and St. Paul) we are not amorphous elements of Christ's Body, like indistinguishable drops of water in the ocean. Rather, we are unique beings that live in him and in the Creator and will forever retain our personal identity in God.[26] God is in all, and each creature will be clearly identifiable *in God.*[27]

True loving union of mind, heart, and spirit, with others and with God, does not absorb or in any way diminish the identity of the members of a union. Relationships personalize people by bringing out more and more of each partner's uniqueness.

As Teilhard puts it, *"Union differentiates."* When you truly enter a relationship, it brings forth qualities and abilities you never realized you had.[28] As players on a basketball team perform their roles during team practice and in competitive games, they develop their unique individual talents and, typically, discover new capabilities in themselves. Likewise, in the Eucharist, each of us becomes a member of a faith team, building our unique talents and developing new ones.

For Teilhard, union also *"super–personalizes"* each member of a union.[29] The team is a "super–person," a new "self" made up of a number of persons. By fully participating in a relationship or a team, each person becomes part of a being greater than himself or herself. The basketball player experiences being part of a *team*. Each one participates in a reality—the team—that is greater than oneself. In the Eucharist, you are being *superpersonalized* by participating in God's very own team—as members of his Body.

Moreover, whatever happens or develops here "in time" does not disappear into a past that exists no longer. Historical persons and events are all kept safe in divine love.[30] For Teilhard, "what happens in time to and through us does not disappear into a past that is no more. Rather, it is preserved in God."[31] We hope and we sense that all is preserved in God.[32]

We trust that nothing good is lost, that all remains alive in God, that all our good actions will themselves continue to live in God who enabled them. Even our well-intentioned actions that failed or fell apart will be kept and treasured by God. The cosmic Eucharist assures us that this is true.

EUCHARIST PRINCIPLE 6:

The Risen Jesus Christ Reveals That the Evolving Physical Universe Is His Body

The Eucharist is a manifestation of the entire Body of Christ.

In any organic body, certain parts of the body cannot be separated from the rest of the body, nor can any parts be separated from the head. They all work together. The entire person, head and body, is the one who acts.

For instance, you may mistakenly assume that it is your arm that writes a letter to a friend. As an imaginary experiment, cut off your writing arm, put a pen in its hand, and put the arm on the writing desk. Nothing happens. Your arm cannot write a letter by itself. It is your whole person that writes a letter.

Similarly, you live as an "arm" of the whole planet. If you think you can live without air, then remove the atmosphere, leaving a vacuum, and see if you can function. If you think you can live without water, then let all the water in your body and on Earth drain away, and see if you can function. If you think your brain and cells can function without ions of metals from the earth like copper, zinc, iron, manganese, and cobalt or minerals like calcium and magnesium, they can't. You also need nuts, fruits, grains, vegetables, and protein to survive. In a word, you cannot live and function without the entire planet. From this perspective, it is not you that lives, but the planet that lives, with you as a part of it.

And so, without Christ bringing love and life to Earth, our planet could not live. Just as we live within the planet, planet Earth lives within Christ. Everything works together, as one organism.

Paul had a glimpse of this reality with Christ as head and source of all creation. To keep us growing and evolving, Christ bestows on humanity many gifts "to equip the saints for the work of ministry, for building up the body of Christ, until all of us come to the unity of the faith and of the knowledge of the Son of God, to maturity, to the measure of the full stature of Christ" (Eph 4:12–13).

Teilhard interprets St. Paul as saying that Christ is indeed head of the Body of the church, that is, all its members.[33] But beyond that, Christ is the head of all creation, that is, everyone and everything else in the universe. Paul writes,

> For the creation waits with eager longing for the revealing of the children of God; for the creation was subjected to futility, not of its own will but by the will of the one who subjected it, in hope that the creation itself will be set free from its bondage to decay and will obtain the freedom of the glory of the children of God. We know that the whole creation has been groaning in labor pains until now; and not only the creation, but we ourselves, who have the first fruits of the Spirit, groan inwardly while we wait for adoption, the redemption of our bodies. (Rom 8:19–23)[34]

Teilhard describes this process in his own words: "Through a vast total made up of infinitely small efforts, through the accumulated effect of rightly directed intention and devotion to the Eucharist, an indestructible world is being built up by our souls and bodies, sheltered by the flesh of Christ."[35] The totality of creation united to Christ as his universal Body constitutes what Paul calls the *Pleroma*. This word evokes a sense of fulfillment or completeness that in Christ all things are held together and filled with his life and love. "For in him the whole fullness of deity dwells bodily, and you have come to fullness in him, who is the head of every ruler and authority" (Col 2:9–10).

In this way, says Teilhard, "the cosmic–Christ becomes cosmically possible. And at the same time, *ipso facto*, he acquires and develops in complete plenitude, a veritable *omnipresence of transformation*. For each one of us, every energy and everything that happens, is superanimated by his influence and his magnetic power."[36] Thus, Christ, in whom dwells the entire cosmos, transforms everything and superanimates everything with his spirit. This Cosmic Christ who lives today is the one we venerate today.

Teilhard's eyes are dazzled as he begins to see how this superanimation enriches our understanding of the Eucharist.

> And then there appears to the dazzled eyes of the believer the eucharistic mystery itself, extended infinitely into a veritable universal transubstantiation, in which the words of the Consecration are applied not only to the sacrificial bread and wine but, mark you, to the whole mass of joys and sufferings produced by the Convergence of the World as it progresses.[37]

What Teilhard is saying is that at the consecration of the host and chalice at eucharistic liturgy, it is not merely Jesus of Nazareth that is brought to life on the altar, but the evolving Cosmic Christ that lives today, including all the joys and suffering happening throughout the world. It is a veritable transubstantiation of everything: Christ the Head cannot be separated from his planetary and Cosmic Body. Even in the words of consecration, the divine Head cannot be separated from his Body.

EUCHARISTIC PRINCIPLE 7:

Jesus Christ as Head of the Body, though Divine, Always Retains His Physicality

The clearest expression of this eucharistic principle of Christ's physicality is found in the tangibility of the Eucharist. By whatever mysterious divine process the eucharistic bread and wine are changed into the body and blood of Jesus Christ,[38] it is clear that *the divine presence is made know to us through things that are physical and accessible to our senses.*

Philosophers and theologians express this eucharistic principle more precisely by saying that in the Eucharist the divine presence is "physically mediated" by the consecrated bread and wine. We understand the need for "physical mediation" of something that is real but not quite tangible. For example, I love my wife. My love for her is very real but my love is not tangible in itself. However, it can be "physically mediated" by something tangible, like a kiss or a hug or even a few loving words.

Normally, when people are face–to–face, they physically mediate their thoughts and feelings through the human voice. When people are not face–to–face, they use their physical cell phones as a medium to communicate feelings, thoughts, information, and plans—all of which are real, but not physical.[39]

For instance, I speak one or more of my intangible pieces of information into my cell phone. My words are mediated through a series of physical electrical impulses, which are sent up to a satellite, then back down to my friend's phone, and there they are decoded into my voice. My nonphysical thoughts are mediated through something physical. We use physical media to convey what is otherwise incommunicable.

The Eucharist is a *medium* that makes Christ accessible, it is not merely a symbol of Christ. A symbol is something that stands for something else. A lily is a symbol of peace, it does not make peace accessible or produce peace. A mascot is a symbol of a sports team, its presence does not make the team accessible or even visible. A crucifix is a symbol of Christ's suffering, it does not make the living Christ accessible or tangible. A symbol merely represents something other than itself. In contrast, *a medium makes the other physically accessible and present.*

Just as we humans make our thoughts or our presence felt *through the medium* of things that are physical and accessible, God makes the divine presence felt *through the medium* of things that are physical and accessible. Using physical realities as a medium of communication is the only access available to a divine nonphysical spiritual being in dealing with physical beings.

The church teaches that, even when the host is divided into many pieces, the whole Christ—body, blood, soul, and divinity—is fully present in every crumb. Similarly, the whole Christ is fully present in every drop of the sacred wine.[40]

Note that a symbol cannot be broken apart. Once broken, a symbol becomes ineffective. A single lily petal does not symbolize peace. Nor does the mascot's boot symbolize the sports team. Nor does a small piece of metal broken off the arm of a crucifix symbolize Christ's suffering. In contrast, every smallest piece of the host is a medium that makes Christ present and available.

We might say that the consecrated host is a fractal, like a mirror. No matter into how many pieces you shatter a mirror, every piece remains a mirror. Similarly, every single cell of your body contains your DNA and reflects you, your complete physical identity. That is why a drop of your saliva studied in a laboratory can identify you. It doesn't merely symbolize you; it *mediates* you. Likewise, each of us *mediates* Christ.

St. Paul described individual believers as "members" of Christ's Body, such as arms, legs, feet, hands, eyes, and ears. Paul knew nothing of cellular biology. Nor did he know that eventually there would be billions of members of Christ's Body. But if he did, he might have described individual humans more like cells in Christ's Body rather than "members." However, both ways of describing elements of Christ's Body are useful.

The value of the cellular image might be that every cell in Christ's Body contains his divine DNA, so that every individual in the Body of Christ can be identified as fully sharing Christ's own lineage. We humans are not mere symbols of Christ's Body; like the Eucharist, we are the medium through which Christ becomes present and accessible on Earth here and now.

We may also say that Christ's DNA may be found in every animal, bird, fish, tree, plant, and flower. Teilhard might go much further and say that Christ's DNA may be found in every subatomic particle that exploded into existence at the Big Bang.

For Paul and Teilhard, everything belongs to Christ and lives in him. He is the "all" in all. If only those who are formally baptized are members of Christ's Body, God's project on Earth remains incomplete. Christogenesis can reach maturity only when all things realize "who" they are a part of.

Some people that have been baptized and are formal members of a Christian community may want to claim that they and only they can be called members of Christ's Body. The Body of Christ contains far more than those who are formally baptized. It includes everyone and everything that can further God's project on Earth.[41]

So, what can Christians uniquely claim because of their baptism?

Christians can uniquely claim a *conscious and professed responsibility* for building the Earth and filling it with love and fuller life. Each day, the baptized faithful recite the Lord's Prayer. In doing so they, in effect, promise God that their most fervent wish for that day is "Thy kingdom come. Thy will be done on Earth." They promise to do their part to make Earth a kingdom of love and unity, "as it is in heaven." Quite a daily responsibility!

EUCHARISTIC PRINCIPLE 8:

The Body of Christ Will Continue to Evolve Until It Achieves Its Total Fullness at the End of Time

This eucharistic principle is concerned with the purpose of human life on Earth in general, and about the purpose of life of each individual person, relationship, and particular group.

Traditionally, Christians believed that God's purpose for creating the universe was to provide a testing ground for humans. Each person would be individually judged or evaluated at death by God. Each would be deemed worthy to enter heaven—or not. In this traditional theological framework, one's specific contributions to society or science—or even to the larger Body of Christ—would have little importance. What was important was how well you as an individual scored on the ultimate "test." You would be graded simply on how carefully you lived your life and avoided sin. In this traditional approach, you lived *on* Earth, but were not *of* it. You were merely a temporary visitor. This traditional moral perspective encouraged you to be kind, compassionate, and forgiving, but offered little motivation for you to put effort into improving human life in general on Earth.

Historically, such a limited perception of one's life purpose might be understandable, since for many centuries most human sweat and struggle was exhaustively spent each day merely on surviving, on just getting through life. During periods of history when life itself was so precarious and short,[42] individuals were counseled to stay focused on making sure they died in the "state of grace" and got to enjoy "eternal rest" in heaven.[43]

In contrast, observing the process of evolution happening everywhere on Earth, Teilhard began to see God's purpose for human life on Earth in a different light. For him, God's purpose in creating—the universe in general and humanity in particular—was *not* to set up a test–for–heaven system, or even to see how well people could avoid the many temptations to sin. God was not out to make humans feel guilty, evil, worthless, and fearful of divine wrath.

Rather, God's purpose was an evolutionary one. God's plan was to have us spend our lives on Earth helping one another—and God—to make our "perfectible" planet an ever–better place in which to live. In other words, God wanted us to spend our lifetime finding ways to love one another ever more deeply so that our planet would eventually become filled with peace and love.

Teilhard pointed out that, from an evolutionary viewpoint, new ways of demonstrating love keep emerging in our planetary family. These new ways emerge through new technology, scientific discoveries, psychological research, advances in knowledge, new patterns of relating, and so on.

Without our effort and creativity in helping transform the world, God not only will not but *cannot* fulfill Jesus's promise to the Father in the Lord's Prayer: "Thy kingdom come. Thy will be done on Earth."

Creaturely tasks can be accomplished only by creatures and not by God independently of those creatures. The moral insight is that human activity is necessary for the building of the world. A house cannot be built by the architect who designed it. To build a house requires the combined work of carpenters, masons, plumbers, electricians, and painters. The Earth cannot be transformed without human beings, individually and in teams, doing their part of the work on God's project. From Teilhard's perspective, God cannot accomplish what God wants to accomplish without our cooperation.[44]

God counts on our dreams, our longings, our creativity and determination in figuring out how to build a loving Earth.[45] Stated more directly, *the will of God is a project to be cocreated with God through the exercise of our human bodies, minds, and hearts.* As workers on God's project, every human person during his or her lifetime on Earth has unique opportunities to contribute in one or more ways to the divine project. The Eucharist is essential to the success of this project, since workers on the divine project need divine nourishment.

EUCHARISTIC PRINCIPLE 9:

The Eucharist Is a Manifestation of the Evolving Body of Christ and Guarantees That the Divine Presence Will Remain among Us until the Divine Project Is Complete

The Eucharist that we receive today is the living body of Jesus Christ, the body as it exists today with everyone and everything in it. Essentially, the Eucharist is always the same divine Person, yet it is somehow new every day.

We experience this evolutionary "newness" in our own being. You and I are always essentially the same person, yet we are also somehow new each day. Our personality has been enriched by our encounters with others and by the events that have happened to us the previous day. Over years and decades of life, our personality has deepened and developed. We would not want others today to treat us as if we were still teenagers. We might reminisce about those high school days and talk about what we knew and didn't know back then, or things we wished we had said or done, but didn't. We might look at old photos and smile at the way we looked, how we wore our hair, or our preference for certain clothes. But that is not the manifestation of who we are today.

And so it is with Christ and the Eucharist. We might like to think of Eucharist in terms of Jesus at the first Christmas, Jesus hanging on the cross, or the risen Jesus on the first Easter. But none of those images represents the Jesus Christ who lives today. None of them reflects his full divine presence on the altar.

The Jesus of Nazareth who once suffered on the cross has become a Person as big as the universe. Jesus is no longer merely thirty years old; he is more like two thousand years old. You may look upon a statue of the crucified Lord hanging above the altar to spark your devotion, but Teilhard says the challenge is to learn to see him as he is today, continually expanding his being and his love far beyond the confines of a church building or even an entire city or town. Today, Christ is cosmic sized.

The becoming of the universe (cosmogenesis) is not simply a series of successive waves of evolutionary progress, nor is Earth's history (geogenesis) merely a story of endless evolution. Both processes have their detours, regressions, and failures. Nevertheless, because of Christ, both cosmogenesis and geogenesis also share a promise of ultimate convergence in a Person (Christogenesis). "What is Our Lord Jesus Christ if not this synthesis of the created Universe and its Creator?"[46] Isn't the Eucharist in fact the *consecration* of this cosmic reality?

The "task" that the eucharistic Christ faces is greater than any individual can imagine or conceive. As members of the Body of Christ, each of us has been "baptized" into a higher life. When you truly enter into life in the Eucharist, you enter into the life of a human–divine Being that is higher than yourself. In this higher life you experience true freedom and you delight in being guided by it. While remaining an individual, you lose your sense of living merely an individual life.

"*Human action* seems to me to be completely satisfying and conscious only when it is carried through in union with the fulfillment of all cosmic perfection," says Teilhard.[47] Humanity's further progress ahead demands primacy of Spirit. Humanity is not merely evolving but *converging*. "Through a vast total made up of infinitely small efforts, through the accumulated effect of rightly directed intention and devotion to the Eucharist, an indestructible world is being built up by our souls and bodies, sheltered by the flesh of Christ."[48]

Teilhard interprets St. Paul as saying that Christ is indeed head of the Body of the church, that is, the head of all its members. But beyond that, Christ is the head of all creation, that is, everyone and everything else in the universe. In its collective consciousness, humanity is coming into the awareness that all of creation is converging into one all–encompassing Person.

The totality of creation united to Christ as his universal Body constitutes what Paul calls the *Pleroma*. *Pleroma* represents the fully mature and perfect Christ, the complete fulfillment of God's divine project.[49]

Divine creation was not finished in seven days, as the Book of Genesis suggests. Creation continues as an ongoing event. It is a divine project still in process. Even today, creation is evolving with a definite direction and purpose toward which God is attracting it from up ahead. God holds a vision of the future—of the "finished product"—on what still needs to be achieved in Christ's Body. For Teilhard, creation is maturing within a divine milieu. It is maturing within the Universal or Cosmic Christ.[50] "To cooperate in total cosmic evolution is the only deliberate act that can adequately express our devotion to an evolutive and universal Christ."[51]

EUCHARISTIC PRINCIPLE 10:

The Eucharist Builds Unity in the Body of Christ and Nourishes Its Members

Sometimes, people think that we receive holy communion merely to celebrate the fact that we are one Body, that we share the same Eucharist to celebrate our oneness. St. Paul says the opposite. In his perception, it is because we continue to share the same Eucharist that we continue to become one Body more and more completely. In Paul's view, our union as believers isn't just celebrated by the Eucharist; in a very real way, our union is being produced and is kept maturing by the Eucharist (see Eph 5:23).

> The cup of blessing that we bless, is it not a sharing in the blood of Christ? The bread that we break, is it not a sharing in the body of Christ? Because there is one bread, we who are many are one body, for we all partake of the one bread. (1 Cor 10:16–17)

> St. John Chrysostom (344–407) says,

> *What is that Bread? The Body of Christ!* What do they become who are partakers therein? They become the Body of Christ! Not many bodies, but one Body....For you are not

58

nourished by this Body while someone else is nourished by that Body; rather, *all are nourished by the same Body*.[52]

The unity of the Body of Christ is grounded, maintained, and nurtured through reception of the Eucharist. According to Tertullian (155–250), "The [human] flesh feeds on the body and blood of Christ, so that the soul too may fatten on God."[53] And St. Clement of Alexandria (150–216) says, "The Lord supplies us with these intimate nutriments. He delivers over his flesh and pours out his blood, and nothing is lacking for the growth of His children. O incredible mystery!"[54]

> Jesus said to them, "I am the bread of life. Whoever comes to me will never be hungry, and whoever believes in me will never be thirsty."
> Those who eat my flesh and drink my blood have eternal life, and I will raise them up on the last day; for my flesh is true food and my blood is true drink. Those who eat my flesh and drink my blood abide in me, and I in them. Just as the living Father sent me, and I live because of the Father, so whoever eats me will live because of me. (John 6:35, 54–57)

It is clear that the New Testament authors believe it is important to show that the Eucharist is central to Jesus's teaching. They understand that it is essential for those who believe in Jesus Christ to continue sharing his body and blood as their spiritual nourishment and as a constant reminder of his living presence among them.

Teilhard would want us to be grounded in how the New Testament authors understand the Eucharist, its meaning and purpose in bringing about the kingdom of God.

3

Eucharist in the New Testament

Sources of the Eucharist

THREE GOSPEL writers — Matthew, Mark, and Luke — describe the scene of the Eucharist's first enactment during the Last Supper, on the night before Jesus suffered and died on the cross. Decades before the three Gospel writers had composed their texts, St. Paul had written to his Corinthian church community commenting about the way they had been celebrating Eucharist (see 1 Cor 11).

Paul assured his Corinthian Christians that weekly celebration of the Lord's Supper was central to their worship and to their very lives as a community of believers. Regular celebration of the Eucharist has been practiced in the church from the beginning.

Although St. Paul had not been present at the Last Supper on Holy Thursday, he assured his Christians that he had the authority to confirm the validity of this eucharistic ritual because *it had been directly revealed to him by Christ* (1 Cor 11:23).

Unlike Matthew, Mark, and Luke, who offer nothing more than the basic facts of the Last Supper story, Paul in 1 Corinthians 11 offers several doctrinal statements about the Eucharist. For example:

- *Jesus himself instituted the form of the eucharistic celebrations* (v. 23).
- "Do this in remembrance of me" *forms the basis of the requirement to attend eucharistic celebrations every Sunday* (v. 24).

- *The eucharistic host and chalice are Jesus Christ, the risen Lord, himself* (v. 27).
- *This risen Christ becomes present whenever we celebrate the Eucharist* (v. 27; see also 1 Cor 12:12, 27).
- *Each of us is a member of Christ's Body, and collectively we make up Christ's Body* (1 Cor 12:12–13).
- *Wherever Christ is present, so is his Body with its members. We — you and I — are with him in the host and chalice* (1 Cor 12:20).
- *The Eucharist re–presents Jesus's sacrifice on the cross* (v. 26).
- *"Until he comes"* assures us that *the Eucharist will continue until the Lord's second coming at the end of time* (v. 26).
- *Serious sin prohibits one from receiving the Eucharist* (v. 27).
- *Examination of conscience and contrition for failures and faults should precede reception of the Eucharist* (vv. 28–29).
- *When you accept the Eucharist in your hand, you must believe that you hold in your hand the living body of Christ* (v. 29).

John's Contributions

Many years later, in the 90s, the apostle John wrote his Gospel. In his retelling of the Last Supper event, John did not include a description of the consecration of the bread and wine. Instead, he had Jesus explain some theological implications of the Eucharist. For example, by using the image of the vine and the branches, Jesus emphasized how he and his followers formed an organic oneness of life — as one Body (see John 15:1–11).

Paul describes how "oneness" with Christ happens in the assembled faithful and in the Eucharist. John adds that the loving oneness between Christ and his Body is meant to become like the loving union Jesus shares with the Father (John 17:21).

John also outlines the Holy Spirit's role in the theology of the Eucharist. He lists the many ways the Holy Spirit would take Jesus's place in their lives by personally guiding them within the Body of Christ (see John 14:15–17, 25–28; 16:12–15). The Holy Spirit would also nurture the oneness of the Body—in the assembly and in the Eucharist.[1]

The believing community, represented by the church fathers, has always acknowledged the Holy Spirit's vital role in the Eucharist.[2] It is the Holy Spirit who changes the bread and wine into the body and blood of Christ at every eucharistic liturgy.

The Lord's Supper

John's Gospel also explains why the apostles were not startled at the Last Supper when Jesus said to them, "This is my body." Much earlier in his Gospel, John had described Jesus's first announcement of the Eucharist (John 6:22–71). In Capernaum, Jesus told the crowds that he would give them his flesh to eat and his blood to drink. On that day, Jesus assured the crowds that he was "the bread that came down from heaven" (John 6:51). He promised also to give them his blood to drink (John 6:53–56).

The apostles had been present in Capernaum when Jesus made this astounding claim. They would remember how this announcement marked a major turning point in Jesus's ministry. On that day, large numbers of his followers walked away, saying, "This teaching is difficult; who can accept it?" (John 6:60). The apostles would remember vividly how, after the crowd had abandoned him, Jesus had turned to them and asked, "Do you also wish to go away?" (John 6:67). But they remained faithful to him. During the Last Supper, when Jesus said, "This is my body" and "This is my blood," they would recall that momentous day in Capernaum when he promised he would give them his flesh and blood as food and drink.

Christ's real presence in the blessed bread and wine has been acknowledged from the beginning.[3]

St. Epiphanius affirmed Christ's presence in the Eucharist with utmost clarity.

We see that the Savior took in His hands, as it is in the Gospel, when He was reclining at the supper; and He took this [the bread], and giving thanks, *He said: "This is really Me."*

And He gave [the cup] to His disciples and said: *"This is really Me."*[4]

Theodore of Mopsuestia offered another way to clarify Jesus's words.

He did not say, "This is the symbol of My Body, and this, of My Blood," but "This is My Body and My Blood," teaching us not to look upon the nature of what is set before us, but that it is transformed by means of the Eucharistic action into Flesh and Blood.[5]

While sharing his final Passover supper with those who had remained faithful to him, Jesus followed through on his promise to give them his flesh to eat and his blood to drink. He would do it under the appearance of bread and wine.

While they were eating, he took a loaf of bread, and after blessing it he broke it, gave it to them, and said, "Take; this is my body." Then he took a cup, and after giving thanks he gave it to them, and all of them drank from it. He said to them, "This is my blood of the [new] covenant, which is poured out for many. Truly I tell you, I will never again drink of the fruit of the vine until that day when I drink it new in the kingdom of God." (Mark 14:22–25)

The institution of the Eucharist presents one of the most evolutionary changes in the history of religions. The Eucharist allows the followers of Jesus to be nourished *daily* with the flesh and blood of their risen and still-living Lord.

In all other religions, the divinity remains distant and remote, inaccessible, and unavailable, requiring great gifts and sacrifices with only the faintest hope of being heard. Jesus painted a totally different picture of God and God's kingdom. He introduced a new kind of God, an interpersonal, welcoming, forgiving, loving God. According to him, God is present, nearby, all around us. In the Eucharist, the Father Creator who is one with Christ becomes totally immediate and accessible, willing to enter our bodies and minds. God's love becomes intimately available.

Frequent, even daily communion was already practiced in the early church as attested to by, for example, St. Cyprian (200–258):

> And we ask that this Bread be given us daily, so that we who are in Christ and daily receive the Eucharist as the food of salvation, may not, by falling into some more grievous sin and then in abstaining from communicating, be withheld from the heavenly Bread, and be separated from Christ's Body.[6]

Wine and Covenant

Each of the four Gospel texts regarding the cup mentions that this ritual of sharing food and wine marks a *covenant* between God and the human family.[7] Covenants form the backbone of the biblical story. Judaism and Christianity are founded on divine covenants.

At its most basic level, a *covenant* describes an oath–bound relationship between two or more parties. A covenant should be distinguished from a *contract*, which is typically about a specific job or *project* and each partner's role in completing the project. When the project is complete, the contract has been fulfilled.

A covenant is not about the accomplishment of a specific project, but about creating a *permanent personal relationship of trust and mutual service between the partners.* The focus is on the relationship. Each side voluntarily promises to uphold the mutually agreed–upon conditions of the relationship.

Many covenants are noted in the history of the Jewish people. We see a variety of them, both human and divine. Typically, human covenants were established between a master and his servants, an employer and his workmen, or a king and his vassals. The most familiar human covenant is marriage between a husband and wife. A divine covenant establishes a relationship between God and his people.

A divine covenant is fundamentally a bond in which God binds himself by his own oath to keep his promises and expects his people to keep their part of the agreement. While God remains faithful to God's promises, the chosen people usually fail to keep theirs.[8] "Whoever, therefore, eats the bread or drinks the cup of the Lord in an unworthy manner will be answerable for the body and blood of the Lord" (1 Cor 11:27).

Most human covenants were formally sealed by the partners during a shared meal. The covenant partners drank a cup of wine together, often from the same cup, as did bride and groom during a wedding feast. In the covenant between Yahweh and the Hebrew people described in Exodus 24, there is an emphasis on eating and drinking (v. 11). We see a similar sharing of a meal in the words and actions of Jesus during the Last Supper.

At the Last Supper, not only does Jesus seal the new covenant in a celebratory meal and by drinking with his disciples from the same cup, he also makes the Eucharist the food and drink that will sustain his followers, including us today, in carrying out our part of the new covenant.[9]

What is especially touching about this new covenant at the Last Supper is that it is being made between human friends. Jesus is not claiming to be God here. He is a man sharing a meal with his friends. He might be saying to them, "I no longer call you servants or disciples, but you are my friends. In fact, you are my brothers, since we have the same Father in heaven" (see John 15:15; cf. Heb 2:11–12). Jesus calls all those who eat and drink of the holy bread and wine his sisters and brothers. Jesus Christ, the divine partner of this covenant, will continue to serve side by side with us in helping to build God's great project of universal salvation.

Some Scripture scholars have found great liturgical significance in Luke's postresurrection story of the risen Jesus meeting a pair of disciples on the road to Emmaus. The story includes—and models—the two key elements of a eucharistic service—Word and Sacrament. First, Jesus "breaks open" the scriptural words as they are walking together on the road. Second, while they were at a meal in the inn, he breaks the bread and shares the eucharistic sacrament with them. He is no longer Jesus of Nazareth but the risen Christ Jesus now presiding over a celebration of Eucharist.

On the very day of his resurrection, the risen Christ is giving us a model of the liturgical actions he wants us to continue doing. On the first Easter Sunday in Emmaus, the risen Christ reenacts the Last Supper ritual of his body and blood with his friends, just as he had instructed his disciples to do and to continue doing. We can imagine that Luke told the Emmaus story again and again in his preaching and when he celebrated Eucharist with small Christian communities. The story showed how Christ wanted us to continue renewing the covenant, and how the risen Christ is really the "celebrant" at every liturgy.

Other Differences

The covenant established by Jesus with his followers is uniquely universal. In the former Mosaic covenant established with the Hebrews, God promised *to protect this people from their enemies*. The new covenant is not about a single nation but the whole world. The new covenant is about carrying out a worldwide divine plan or project that Jesus called the reign of God. In the new covenant, both God and the people commit themselves to this work: *bringing salvation, or the fullness of life, to the whole world*. "I came that they may have life, and have it abundantly" (John 10:10).

The new covenant represents a partnership in this saving work between God and his people. In his public life, Jesus assured us that the building of God's kingdom on Earth could go forward with confidence because *God offered complete forgiveness of the sins of the people*. Jesus willingly died for the sins of all humans, so that, free from fear of punishment for sin, we could completely dedicate ourselves to building the kingdom of God on Earth.

This new covenant reveals still another difference. At the Last Supper, Jesus established a traditional yet startlingly new bond with God's people in a ritual that provided *immediate access to God* that had not been available in the old covenant.

The first clear statement of this new covenant can be found early in John's Gospel: "For God so loved the world that he gave his only Son, so that everyone who believes in him might not perish but might have eternal life" (John 3:16). Believing in Jesus involves more than a simple intellectual profession of faith; belief calls for a *life spent following Jesus's way in word and action*. The very next sentence in this passage restates and confirms the positive content of the new covenant: "God did not send the Son into the world to condemn the world, but in order that the world might be saved through him" (John 3:17).

The word *saved*, or *salvation*, is a process word. *Salvation* might best be translated as "enjoying the fullness of life." Salvation is a healing and wholeness process of inner vitality. For humanity, salvation begins and is enriched during life on Earth, and it will continue to grow consciously forever with God in heaven. Jesus emphasized his mission of salvation by saying, "I came that they may have life, and have it abundantly" (John 10:10). Salvation means much more than being saved from sin; it is primarily about enjoying the fullness of life.

During the Last Supper and after they share the blessing cup, Jesus says to them, "Truly I tell you, I will never again drink of the fruit of the vine until that day when I drink it new in the kingdom of God" (Mark 14:25).[10] "That day" will begin on Easter Sunday, when in his risen state he reveals his full identity as Jesus the Christ, Lord of the Universe. And, in his new glorified state, he manifests the fullness of life displayed in all its magnificence.

Each eucharistic liturgy is a renewal of the new covenant. In reciting the Lord's Prayer together before holy communion, we renew aloud this covenant. We specify God's part as well as our part in it. We promise to do all we can to complete God's project. We say, "Thy kingdom come. Thy will be done on Earth."

Then, as you and I receive the Eucharist we, individually and collectively, publicly ratify this new covenant and affirm to the world that we commit ourselves to its work. To realize that during each liturgy we are reaffirming the covenant made at the Last Supper gives us great energy to live for Christ.

John's Theology of the Eucharist

The other three Gospel writers present the institution of the Eucharist as a ritual to be reenacted again and again in memory of Jesus. The Gospel writers present only the story. St. Paul offers some theology as well.[11] But early Christians had to wait, perhaps thirty years after Paul, for the Gospel of John to develop more fully the deeper theology behind this transformational process.

John's Gospel develops the meaning, purpose, and significance of the Eucharist. At the Last Supper, during his final discourse, Jesus describes the personal and communal process of building a loving community among humans and with God. He explains how it will operate. The centerpiece of the process and the guarantee of its success is Jesus's command that his followers love one another with the deep and forgiving love that he showed for them.

> This is my commandment, that you love one another as I have loved you. No one has greater love than this, to lay down one's life for one's friends. You are my friends if you do what I command you. I do not call you servants any longer, because the servant does not know what the master is doing; but I have called you friends, because I have made known to you everything that I have heard from my Father. You did not choose me but I chose you. And I appointed you to go and bear fruit, fruit that will last, so that the Father will give you whatever you ask him in my name. I am giving you these commands so that you may love one another. (John 15:12–17)

With the confirmation of John's theology, Paul's mystical Body of Christ cannot be interpreted as a mere metaphor—like membership in a corporation or citizenship in a country. John's theology asserts the physical and spiritual reality of the Christ Body.

> Those who eat my flesh and drink my blood abide in me, and I in them. Just as the living Father sent me, and I live because of the Father, so whoever eats me will live because of me. (John 6:56–57)

Because of this intimate union, we live in Christ's Body, much as living cells share in the life of any organism. This participation in Christ's Body also allows us to "think and act" with the mind of Christ.[12] It also allows us to claim to live in Christ and act on behalf of Christ.

From Teilhard's perspective, John's presentation of Jesus's farewell address during the Last Supper describes the ultimate divine unification of all things. It describes the accomplishment of God's project. It is what Teilhard called the Omega Point[13] and St. Paul called the *Pleroma* (see Col 2:9; Eph 4:13).[14]

Jesus's prayer to the Father includes all humanity, not just the people around him at the Last Supper. He prays that all may be sanctified in the truth. Moreover, he prays that *all humanity may become one with him and his Father*. Jesus envisions a long future of believers:

I ask not only on behalf of these, but also on behalf of those who will believe in me through their word, that they may all be one. As you, Father, are in me and I am in you, may they also be one in us, so that the world may believe that you have sent me. (John 17:20–22)

In the time of Jesus, Jews claimed to be "children of Abraham" because they could trace their bloodline back to Abraham. John explained that Jesus was initiating a new "bloodline." Through the eucharistic meal, his followers would continue to receive a spiritual blood transfusion. Collectively, they will gradually evolve into a new kind of being as each one becomes more and more like Jesus. John described this process of becoming one with Jesus and the Father.

To indicate this oneness, John uses the image of the vine and the branches. Jesus is the vine, whose roots send their life–giving energy into its branches. Those living in his "vine" generate delicious fruit (John 15:1–11).

Paul uses a different image to express this intimate union. For him, those who follow Jesus's way—who eat his flesh and drink his blood—become part of a much larger, cosmic–sized Christ. They become members—eyes, arms, legs, et cetera—of this grand Christ Body (1 Cor 12:15–27). Since there are so many millions—or even billions—of us living in Christ's Body, a more contemporary image to describe those who follow Jesus's way might be as "living cells" in his universal Body.

Only in John and Paul do we find this grand evolution in theology.

Eucharist and Cosmic Life

Ordinary bread gives nourishment. True bread gives life. Eucharist is the true bread of life. It is the bread of eternal life. Since this bread is the flesh of a divine body, it gives a share in divine life. Because Christ is everywhere and eternal, the Eucharist becomes the bread of cosmic life. Since Christ's divine Body is the body of the cosmos, this bread gives cosmic life. If you live within Christ, you inhabit the entire cosmos. Likewise, if you live anywhere in the cosmos, you live within Christ.

Christ in the Eucharist isn't simply Jesus of Nazareth. At the resurrection, God gave Jesus of Nazareth a new role, an evolved life to live. As Peter, inspired by the Holy Spirit on Pentecost Day, said, "God has made him both Lord and Messiah, this Jesus" (Acts 2:36).

A cosmic notion of Christ competes with no one and excludes no one but embraces in love everything and everyone, "that they may all be one. As you, Father, are in me and I am in you, may they also be one in us, so that the world may believe that you have sent me" (John 17:21).

When you partake of the eucharistic bread, you agree to enter the Body of Christ and live there. Consciously. You also agree to be involved in maintaining and developing the life of this evolving universal Body—to care for it, to accept responsibility for its health and growth. In consciously choosing to be a member of this universal Body, you accept a big responsibility—for your own physical body, for the believing community, for all humans, for our planet, and for the cosmos.

We have not yet assumed our full responsibility.

For example, people and governments in general have not assumed responsibility for caring for Earth's health. We continue to exploit Earth for its natural resources and energy resources in order to make a small group of people rich. We are not enriching our planet with life but, in a million sins of omission, we are simply watching it die.

It is the role of the Christian who accepts responsibility for the health of Christ's Cosmic Body to reverse this destructive pattern and the exploitation of nature. Many, including Pope Francis, believe that caring for Earth, our home, should be a primary focus of our efforts at this crucial time in our planet's history.[15]

It is not a big leap to say that Pope Francis, in his planetary and cosmic perspective, is merely echoing his fellow Jesuit, Teilhard. Teilhard also makes a clear connection between this cosmic perspective and the eucharistic liturgy. As Teilhard writes in *Christianity and Evolution,* "The greatest change [in our perspective of the world], however, comes with mass and communion, when we realize the full depth and universality of their mystery."[16] For Teilhard, the celebration of mass is a cosmic event.

We now understand that, when Christ descends sacramentally into each one of his faithful, it is not simply in order to commune with him; it is in order to join him, physically, a little more closely to himself and to all the rest of the faithful, in the growing unity of the world. When, through the priest, Christ says, "This is my body," the words reach out infinitely far beyond the morsel of bread over which they are pronounced: they bring the entire mystical body into being. The priestly act extends beyond the transubstantiated Host to the cosmos itself, which, century after century, is gradually being transformed by the Incarnation, itself never complete.[17]

For St. Paul, this is the Christ who always carries with him his entire Body of humans as well as the cosmos. As St. Paul says of Christ,

He is the image of the invisible God, the firstborn of all creation; for in him all things in heaven and on earth were created, things visible and invisible…all things have been created through him and for him…and in him all things hold together. He is the head of the body….For in him all the fullness of God was pleased to dwell, and through him God was pleased to reconcile to himself all things, whether on earth or in heaven. (Col 1:15–20)

Teilhard continually stressed this cosmic aspect of Christ and the Eucharist. He hoped to bring forward both the Eucharist's cosmic sense as well as its evolutionary quality as central themes in the Christian view of reality. He struggled to express these ideas in terms of his tradition. He knew that the cosmic idea was essential to Paul's theology and to that of the early doctors of the church.

Yet, the church of Teilhard's day in its fear and distrust of modern science remained focused on a theology that not only asserted that the opening chapters of Genesis were scientifically accurate. It also claimed that the world was "enemy" and promoted a very self–centered spirituality. In this tradition, receiving the Eucharist was an exclusively personal event between me and Jesus. No one else was invited into my intimate communion space. Certainly not the rest of the congregation. Certainly not the worldwide Christian family. And certainly not the universe.

Teilhard wanted people to recognize the cosmic dimensions of the Eucharist. As he explained,

From age to age, there is but one single [continual eucharistic liturgy being celebrated] in the world: the true Host, the total Host, is the universe which is continually being more intimately penetrated and vivified by Christ. From the most distant origin of things until their unforeseeable consummation, through the countless convulsions of boundless space, the whole of nature is slowly and irresistibly undergoing the supreme consecration. Fundamentally—since all time and for ever—but one single thing is being made in creation: the body of Christ.[18]

Teilhard was making a powerful connection. For the very first time, here was a scientist–theologian showing his church how to integrate science's evolutionary cosmology with theology's Universal Christ. Unfortunately, few in the church would listen. Of those who were willing to listen, many failed to grasp Teilhard's understanding of the Eucharist. Few, too, were those who could grasp a Christ who was both here and now with us, yet at the same time waiting for us up ahead and beckoning us to evolve toward him.

4

The Evolving Christ

Christ Up Ahead

TEILHARD'S APPROACH to the risen Christ and to the Eucharist is unique because he includes in both the future Christ. Teilhard shines the spotlight on the Christ who is still becoming, still growing toward his fulfillment at the end of time.

Many of us are very aware of the *Christ who was*, namely, Jesus of Nazareth.

Some are becoming more clearly aware of the *Christ who is*, namely, the Mystical Body of Christ that lives today.

For Teilhard there is also the *Christ who will be*.

Even though the *Christ who was* is no longer walking on Earth, Christ presently is both *with us* (alongside) and *up ahead of us*, beckoning us forward, inviting us to grow in love, individually and as a people.

The idea of someone who is both *with us* and *up ahead of us* is a familiar experience. For example, schoolteachers are both *with* their pupils as well as *up ahead of* them. Students are being invited to learn new knowledge and develop new skills that their teachers are waiting to impart. Parents are both *with* and *up ahead* of their young children urging them to grow and develop skills that their parents already have and know that their children will need.

In traditional prayer, we were seldom taught to picture the cosmic Christ either *alongside* us or *up ahead*, beckoning us forward, individually and collectively, urging us to grow up. We tended to keep our prayer imagery fixed on the *Christ who was*, namely Jesus of Nazareth. However, when we contemplate the Eucharist in its fullness, we discover there not only the *Christ who was* and the *Christ who is today*, but

73

also, as Teilhard likes to say, the *Christ up ahead*. For many, the last two realities of Christ provide new dimensions for exploring eucharistic spirituality.

The Mystical Body of Christ that lives *today* on Earth has been growing in size and consciousness for two thousand years. The *Christ with us* has developed significantly from his time as Jesus of Nazareth until now.

Eucharistic spirituality almost never considers the *Christ who will be*, though its importance can be traced back to St. Paul's letters and the writings of John the Evangelist. Teilhard says that we need seriously to consider these often–forgotten dimensions of the Eucharist in our liturgy and spirituality.

For many, it may require a big leap in spiritual practice, to jump from *praying to the Christ who was*, to praying *from within the Christ who is* and, in a further jump, *praying into the Christ who will be*. With Teilhard's help, the transformation can happen more easily if we do it in two stages.

A First *Metanoia*

At a first stage in evolutionary thinking, Teilhard encourages us to begin seeing in the Eucharist the Christ who lives *today* in his universal Body. In this, Teilhard echoes St. Paul who was trying to get his new Christians to realize a number of facts. Paul told them—and us—that by baptism,

- We share Christ's very life as members of Christ's Body.
- Individually, we live each day *in* Christ's Body.
- Our community *as a community* also lives with Christ and in Christ.
- We live *alongside* Christ during our daily activities.
- We live in the Eucharist.

To accomplish the first stage jump from relating to the Christ who was to awareness of the Christ who is requires a *metanoia*.

Metanoia, in general, means shifting one's way of thinking from a more restrictive mindset to one that is more open and more inclusive.

Noia is Greek for "mindset" or "way of thinking or perceiving." *Meta* is Greek for "higher" or "more open" or "more comprehensive." To be able to see the Christ who is requires that we put on a new mindset that is more comprehensive and all–encompassing.

People individually undergo *metanoia* several times in life. Examples of acquiring more inclusive viewpoints (*metanoia*) occur in the educational process from elementary school through college. Each new stage of learning produces broader or more comprehensive ways of thinking and perceiving. Getting married and especially accepting responsibility for raising children requires learning new ways of thinking and widening of consciousness (*metanoia*). Spiritual conversion is still another example of *metanoia*.

Listen to Paul as he greets his Corinthian assembly at the beginning of his letter. He is trying to get them to realize that they live in the Christ who lives today, and that their true life is life within this Christ who is. In the quote below, I have highlighted the many times that Paul sees his people as living in this new reality; he sees them as *living in Christ* and as changed and enriched because they live in Christ.

> To the church of God that is in Corinth, to those who are sanctified *in Christ Jesus*, called to be saints, *together with all* those who in every place call on the name of our Lord Jesus Christ, both their Lord and ours: Grace to you and peace from God our Father and the Lord Jesus Christ.
>
> I give thanks to my God always for you because of the grace of God that has been given you *in Christ Jesus*, for in every way you have been enriched [by living] *in him*, in speech and knowledge of every kind—just as the testimony of Christ has been strengthened among you—so that you are not lacking in any *spiritual gift* as you wait for the revealing of our Lord Jesus Christ. He will also *strengthen you* to the end, so that you may be blameless on the day of our Lord Jesus Christ. God is faithful; *by him* you were called into the *fellowship* of his Son, Jesus Christ our Lord. (1 Cor 1:2–9, emphasis added)

Paul tried to get his people to realize that they were not just a collection of people who believed in Christ and followed his teachings. They had become so much more, individually and as a group. In baptism, Paul told them, they died to their old life and the way they saw themselves and were reborn into Christ and into a new way of seeing themselves. In this rebirth, they emerged, organically, as new beings, as members (cells, atoms) in Christ's Cosmic Body. They were no longer just ordinary human beings. He said, "Now you are the body of Christ and individually members of it" (1 Cor 12:27).

For Paul, this incorporation into Christ is not merely a spiritual incorporation but a physical one as well. We have not merely put on the *mind of Christ*; we have become *his very physical Body*. For instance, in condemning fornication, Paul says very clearly, "Do you not know that your bodies are members of Christ?" (1 Cor 6:15). And again: "Or do you not know that your body is a temple of the Holy Spirit within you, which you have from God, and that you are not your own?" (1 Cor 6:19).

> For just as the body is one and has many members, and all the members of the body, though many, are one body, so it is with Christ. For in the one Spirit we were all baptized into one body—Jews or Greeks, slaves or free—and we were all made to drink of one Spirit. (1 Cor 12:12–13)

Additionally, Paul says to the Romans,

> For as in one body we have many members, and not all the members have the same function, so we, who are many, are one body in Christ, and individually *we are members one of another*. (Rom 12:4–5)

As members of one another in Christ's body, we live alongside one another and cooperate with one another. We enjoy a shared life in one great organism, a life that is physical as well as spiritual.

Moreover, Paul told them that, each time they shared Eucharist with each other, they were receiving not merely Christ's head or spirit, but also his body. Head and Body. At the Last Supper, Christ did not say over the bread, "This is my spirit," but rather, "This is my body— the whole me."

The same is true also of the Eucharist that we receive at liturgy today. Christ's Body always includes his universal Body. They cannot be separated. A head cannot live without the body, nor can the body live without its head. Receiving holy communion affirms and confirms us as a whole community of believers living physically in the Body of Christ.

If Christ incorporates us into his body at baptism, then we are members of his body in the Eucharist. If we live in Christ's universal Body today, we must also live in the Eucharistic Body today. Whoever lives in the Universal Christ also lives in the Eucharist, as is clearly acknowledged in the Eucharistic Prayer in the liturgy. There, it is described as a kind of "second transubstantiation."[1]

After the consecration of the Host, the priest says, *"Grant that we, who are nourished by His body and blood, may be filled with his Holy Spirit, and become one body, one spirit in Christ."*[2]

A More Open and Inclusive Spiritual Life

If we are, together, members of Christ's Body, we can no longer keep our spiritual lives self–focused and self–enclosed. We need to develop a collective spiritual life that extends beyond the liturgical celebration. The Eucharist becomes a good model for nurturing this collective existence in our daily lives.

To remain self–focused, while living in a greater body, would be like your lung saying to your body, "I don't care that you want oxygen, body, I am concerned only about myself and my welfare. I couldn't care less about the nourishment that your heart or brain may need from me to function. I just want to focus on myself and my well–being."

Getting us to think of ourselves as living within Christ is a huge step in spirituality. St. Paul's Christian community had to make the step. He tells them,

> From now on, therefore, we regard no one from a human point of view [literally, "according to the flesh"]; *even though we once knew Christ from a human point of view, we know him no longer in that way*. So if anyone is in Christ, there is a new creation: everything old has passed away; see, everything has become new! (2 Cor 5:16–17, emphasis added)

It appears that the Corinthian community had a few older individuals who knew Jesus of Nazareth in Judea "according to the flesh." For

77

Paul, this was of no great importance. He is trying to get his people to see themselves as a new creation. They are no longer mere individual human beings living separate individual lives. They're part of a greater body. They also need to let go of seeing themselves as praying to Jesus of Nazareth *as to another human being*, now in heaven. Paul wants his people to cease seeing themselves as individuals walking on the planet. They have been born into a new life in the resurrected Christ. For them to realize this new perspective is what is most important to Paul. They are now living in Christ's universal Body. They need to see themselves, individually and together, sharing life in the *Christ who is*. The new challenge is to learn *to pray from within Christ and in Christ's name*. In the eucharistic liturgy, they are to see themselves together in the Host—as Christ's Body—praying to the Father. Paul was trying to get his young community to experience the first *metanoia*, the shift of focus from the Christ who was to the Christ who is.

Remember that it would be twenty or more years later before any of the Gospels appeared. The Gospels would offer to future genera-tions access to many of Jesus's sayings and healings that Paul had never heard. Paul seldom mentioned events from the public life of Jesus, since he hadn't witnessed any of them. His focus was not on the Christ who was but on the Christ who is.

What, then, is the value of the gospel stories to us? As one author uniquely put it, "Jesus [of Nazareth] spent a lifetime becoming Christ. How do I best learn from him?"[3] Knowing the words and actions of the Christ who was can prove very helpful for those who want guidance on how to live more effectively in the Christ who is.

Teilhard, being brought up in a self–focused spirituality that was focused on Christ who was, needed to make this first step, just as Paul's people did—and as we need to do. We need to undergo the first *meta-noia* and learn to pray from within the Christ who is. This is different from praying *to Christ*. Of course, we may pray from both perspectives.

Remember, too, that the Christ who is also includes the Christ who was, just as the you who lives now carries with you the *you who was*. The *you who is* carries your entire history.

This first *metanoia* includes not only a new way to pray, but also a new way to think and act in daily life. We need to realize, as Paul's community did, that because we live in the Christ who is, we need to learn to act as his members. We are the eyes and ears of Christ, the hands and feet of Christ. How few of us truly grasp that we are a *new creation*, which needs to learn to pray from within Christ and that needs to learn to think and act like Christ. We need to learn to look at the Eucharist and see Christ as he is today, with all of us as part of his Cosmic Body. He is the head and we are his Body.

Christ's Body today is no longer simply the physical body that Jesus had in Nazareth. Christ today is no more living in that finite male body, than you or I are still living in the body we had when we were children.

This is the first *metanoia* that we undergo in approaching the Eucharist—living, acting, and praying from within the Christ who is. Without entering this higher way of thinking, we remain limited in our old habits of perception. Because of these old habits, we may miss seeing Christ who is right in front of us—and in whom we live and move and have our being.

Metamorphosis and Endomorphisms

Our inhibitions, indoctrinations, and habits "often prevent us from recognizing what is staring us in the face," said Teilhard. It took him a long time before he could see what was staring him in the face.

> I failed to understand that as God "metamorphized" the World from the depths of matter to the peaks of Spirit, so in addition the world must inevitably and to the same degree "endomorphize" God.[4]

Teilhard often shares powerful insights like this that are difficult to grasp at first reading. In this one sentence he captures the essence of his theology of Christ and of the Eucharist, without naming either. In addition, he inserts into his theological vocabulary, without warning, two concepts—*metamorphosis* and *endomorphism*—that are unfamiliar to most people who aren't biologists or mathematicians.

Metamorphosis is something different from and beyond *metanoia*. Both Greek terms have *meta* in their roots. *Noia* means mindset or way of thinking. *Morph* means form or shape. *Metanoia* means to adopt a higher way of thinking. Metamorphosis means to take on a higher form or become a more complex structure, in other words, *to evolve in form. Metanoia* makes possible a higher way of thinking. In metamorphosis you grow to become a higher, more evolved being. *Metanoia* enables you to see and comprehend more. Metamorphosis allows you to be and do more.

Metamorphosis describes an evolutionary process. A familiar example is a caterpillar undergoing a metamorphosis. In becoming a butterfly, a caterpillar morphs into a higher form. Today, we would say that the caterpillar is hardwired for that transformation. Teilhard's point is that just as a caterpillar is genetically programmed to morph into a higher form, so are we. We are hardwired for the transformation into this new life, except that we must learn to use our inner wiring consciously. We need to apply elements of this genetic program that we haven't explored before to initiate the transformation. The entire universe, over billions of years, has been hardwired to undergo a continuing metamorphosis.

At the Big Bang, the universe began its earliest stage as an explosion of purely inert matter. Since then, it has metamorphosed into atoms and molecules, then into stars and planets. On Earth, matter has metamorphosed into oceans full of primitive living cells; then into a planet teeming with sea creatures; next into continents full of flora and fauna; then into valleys, plains, and hills full of moving land animals with sight, smell, hearing, and the ability to reproduce and evolve. With humanity, God watched Earth metamorphose into a planet enveloped in thought, consciousness, and spirit.

Teilhard is not afraid to say that the drive to metamorphosis was built into the universe at the Big Bang. God invented metamorphosis. God implanted the drive to metamorphosis in all of creation. God created a universe that is hardwired to keep metamorphing and evolving. That's some of what Teilhard meant when he realized, "I failed to understand that...God 'metamorphized' the World [the universe] from the depths of matter to the peaks of Spirit." Implied in Teilhard's words is that, with our conscious cooperation and energy, God wants to continue the process and metamorphize us even further.

The rest of Teilhard's difficult sentence reads, "In addition the world [humanity] must inevitably and to the same degree 'endomorphize' God." We can acknowledge that Teilhard is describing our *necessary response* to the discovery that God made metamorphosis—and evolution—the most powerful and universal processes in the universe.

80

But what is the function of an *endomorphism*? And what does it mean to endomorphize God?

Endomorphism

In science, an endomorphism is a new way of mapping a familiar reality. A new mapping enables people to see what they could not see clearly with a previous map.

For example, I keep an up–to–date street map of Tampa in my car. It is the only mapping I need to find my way to almost any address in the city. However, the power company's electrician tracing a power outage needs a different map of Tampa, one that describes the city's electrical grid including transfer stations. The electrician's mapping of Tampa is an endomorphism. It maps the same territory as my street map, but, when placed over my street map, reveals things to the electrician that my street map does not provide.

The water and sewer map of Tampa creates another endomorphism, important for civil engineers and sanitation people. Each television cable company needs its own mapping of the city, as does the environmental team who maps the water table beneath the earth and flood zones of the city. Each new mapping of Tampa is an endomorphism.

Each of these new mappings, or endomorphisms, enables people to see what they could not see clearly with other maps.

In terms of the universe, science has mapped the beginnings and development of the cosmos. Their mappings reveal stages in the evolutionary process from the Big Bang of inert matter over billions of years ago, to its present state of a planet where consciousness and spirit have come to dominate. This is a map that science made and continues to update. There is nothing wrong with this map, says Teilhard, except that it shows only one perspective, science's viewpoint.

I should point out that maps sometimes lose some of their usefulness. I happen to have a street map of Tampa printed fifty years ago. Today, it is an inadequate and misleading relic, since there are hundreds more streets now that are unaccounted for on my old map.

Similarly, the map of a static, fixed, but cyclical universe that cosmologists used in previous centuries has become quite inadequate to explain the evolving universe that we now know. The creation story in the first chapters of the Book of Genesis is another example of an inadequate mapping of the cosmos.[5] Neither of these mappings revealed the numerous metamorphoses that happened to the universe throughout its multibillion–year history. They're like my fifty–year–old, outdated street map of Tampa.

Even in theology and spirituality, we need to design new maps, or at least to update the maps we currently use.

Teilhard wants to introduce a new mapping, *a new endomorphism*. This is a map that describes the beginnings and development of the universe *from God's perspective*.

Teilhard does not want to do away with science's mapping. He merely wants to place his theological mapping on top of the map science has developed. In this way, we see that both maps, as different as they may seem, are mapping the same reality. Each mapping (endomorphism) reveals things that enrich the other mapping. They are both giving us valuable information.

Imagine that Teilhard's map is sketched on a transparent sheet of plastic, so that in looking down at it, you can clearly see the lines of science's mapping below Teilhard's map. Both are different mappings of the same reality: the development of the universe. Each provides information from a different perspective. Science's mapping emphasizes evolution's physical changes. Teilhard's mapping emphasizes how the development of the universe and Earth reveal the nature and personality of God. His mapping identifies how God has been involved in the metamorphosis of matter throughout the same multibillion–year period.[6] Teilhard's endomorphism is a mapping of the evolution of love, consciousness, and faith.

Perhaps now we can better understand Teilhard's sentence that may have been incomprehensible earlier:

> I failed to understand that as God "metamorphized" the World [universe] from the depths of matter to the peaks of Spirit, so in addition the world [humanity] must inevitably and to the same degree "endomorphize" God.[7]

We need to study Teilhard's new mapping and see what we can learn from it in relating to Christ and the Eucharist, and especially in how Christ and the Eucharist relate to each other.

The Unitive Process

Teilhard's mapping (endomorphism) of creation's story shows clearly that *a unitive process* guided by God has been operating all along, beginning from the Big Bang.[8] The divine mapping describes a process that keeps bringing things into higher and higher unities. In our age, God is fostering the universe's latest stage of metamorphosis, since today's human race needs to undergo a new change of form. This transformation process is designed to unify humanity into one close-knit and loving family. It is a process of convergence.

The Eucharist not only fosters present unity, it continually calls for deeper and wider unity. According to Paul, through the Eucharist we are not only being incorporated into Christ. We are thereby being incorporated into God. In Teilhard' words, "As a direct consequence of the unitive process by which God is revealed to us, he in some way 'transforms himself' as he incorporates us."[9]

Even as the Cosmic Christ transforms us—incorporates us into himself—Christ is being "transformed." More precisely, Christ is transforming himself and us. He is the same Christ, yet he becomes somehow new each day. Again, in Teilhard's words,

> All around us, and within our own selves, God is in process of "changing," as a result of the coincidence of his magnetic power and our own Thought. As the "Quantity of cosmic Union" rises, so his brilliance increases and the glow of his coloring grows richer.[10]

In simpler language, Teilhard is saying something like: "For me, every day at the liturgy there is a 'new' Christ on the altar, changed and different from the Christ that was there the day before because, during the past day, the Christ Body has suffered, learned, grown, and evolved just a little bit more all over the Earth."

No longer can we envision just Jesus of Nazareth in the Eucharist. The Eucharist contains and reveals so much more. All of us are in the blessed bread and wine—not just believers, but everyone, as well as all the animals, flowers, and the planet itself. The Eucharist holds it all.

83

Another *Metanoia*

To make the first step in eucharistic spirituality—shifting primacy of focus from the Christ who was to the Christ who is—is a lot to ask of many believers. For Teilhard, this first step is not enough. He invites us even further.

He proposes to us another advance, another shift in the way we view the Eucharist. He wants us to realize what the Eucharist can be in its fullness. He wants us also to begin seeing in the Eucharist the Christ who will be. This is the Christ up ahead, the Christ who is inviting us as a people to evolve in love so that we who are his Body become more and more like him, our Head.

Learning how to think and act from the perspective of the Christ up ahead becomes the new challenge. For Teilhard, this invitation to see Christ up ahead of us reveals the true force of holy communion.

As Teilhard studied the gradual emergence of *Homo sapiens* through eons of time, he was able to recognize "the rise within my own self of the forces of Communion. Everything was directed towards the intensification of the Stuff of the cosmos, so that in that Stuff the Presence of God might be intensified for me."[11]

The Christ who will be knows what the Father Creator wants of us. When we pray in the Lord's Prayer "Thy kingdom come," Christ up ahead knows what the *kingdom–that–will–be* is meant to look like at its fulfillment. It will be a kingdom where love rules and all people love one another. What Jesus was teaching us two thousand years ago, and what Paul could envision, was an even higher stage of metamorphosis than what is happening in our age.[12]

What does the Christ who will be require of us? What is our responsibility? Teilhard says,

> It is no longer a matter of seeing Him and allowing oneself to be enveloped and penetrated by Him—we have to do more. We have…to disclose Him (or even in one sense of the word to "complete" Him) ever more fully. Such, today, seems to me the essential step to be taken by hominized Evolution, and such is its essential concern.[13]

For Teilhard, "hominized Evolution" refers to the evolutionary process that has generated self–reflective *Homo sapiens* and sees our species evolving toward higher and higher consciousness. In other words, we humans now know that, throughout the universe, evolution is the process that is shaping everything everywhere and in all fields of knowledge. Once we self–reflective beings have grasped the laws of evolution and learned to work with them, we can begin to assume a level of responsibility for the success of evolution, for the success of God's project. The Christ who will be knows what the final desired outcome of the divine project will be.

One part of the covenant we made with God, as Teilhard sees it, is to "disclose" God and the fulfillment of the kingdom of God (God's project) to the world. To "disclose" means to make known some secret or new information. The "secret" about God that had been hidden from us until recently is the prevalence of evolution and how God is using evolution to bring about the kingdom of God on Earth.

Now that humans understand evolution, how it works, and how it reveals to us things about God, we can make known to others (disclose) information about God that we never knew two centuries ago. Thanks to modern science, we can reveal a great secret about God that we could never have recognized before discovering the dynamics of evolution.

"God of the Above" and "God of the Ahead"

Now that we know how evolution works, its trajectory and goal, we are ready to undergo a second *metanoia*. Teilhard describes how he entered this second *metanoia*, this new mindset:

> I could see one thing: that, from the depths of the cosmic future as well as from the heights of Heaven, it was still God, it was *always the same God* who was calling me. It was a *God of the ahead* who had suddenly appeared athwart [i.e., across from] *the traditional God of the Above*, so that henceforth we

can no longer worship fully unless we superimpose those two images so that they form *one*.[14]

Teilhard is describing a new endomorphism, the overlapping mapping of two images—*God of the above* and *God of the ahead*—so that we can see that they reveal the same reality.

The God of the above is the supernatural God who dwells in heaven. The God of the ahead is the God on Earth calling us toward him. We can attain him only by evolving—as a species—beyond our present state of consciousness to an ultrahuman state, to the conscious recognition of God within each of us. This process is nothing more than a continuation of Teilhard's law of Complexity–Consciousness.

Traditional spirituality focused exclusively on the God of the above, that is, God in heaven. When people held a fixed cosmic mindset, the meaning and workings of the kingdom of God were all about avoiding sin and getting into heaven. In that mindset, there was no need to transform Earth. We were aliens here. The spiritual challenge was to survive and, at physical death, to return to our true home (heaven), where we are with the God of the above. In the fixed cosmic mindset, this described the process of "salvation."

Evolution–centered spirituality includes a focus on the God of the ahead. It enriches the description of salvation. Our present spiritual challenge is to work with each other and with Christ to transform (evolve) our birth home (Earth) so that it provides to all of us and to future generations more and more fullness of life and love (salvation). The God of the ahead (on Earth) and the God of the above (in heaven) both beckon us to keep evolving toward the fullness of divine life (salvation) that will be achieved when God's project is complete.[15]

Both images—the God of the ahead and the God of the above—are of the same God. Both may be found in the Eucharist: the Christ who sits at the right hand of the Father in heaven, and the Christ who beckons us to work with him in creating a transformed future for Earth.

Teilhard wrote, "I now see with a vision that will never leave me what the World is desperately in need of at this very moment, if it is not to collapse."[16] Our world needs this "vision" (that Christ Ahead offers) of the *Pleroma* plus the will to make it real. The Eucharist nourishes us in this regard. To make the vision real, says Teilhard, we need a "propulsive faith" that drives us forward, and a "new Charity in which all the Earth's dynamic passions combine as they are divinized."[17]

The Evolving Christ

Teilhard says to Christ in the Eucharist, "You have become for my mind and heart much more than He who was and is; you have become *He who shall be*."[18]

Teilhard's God is "no longer the God of the old [fixed] Cosmos but the God of the new *Cosmogenesis*."[19] Christ has come into a universe that is no longer viewed as a cosmos static and finished. He has come into and is in charge of managing a universe that is continually being born anew, a world that is coming to realize ever more and more its fullest potential. It is Jesus Christ who brings this *God the Evolver* to us. Here is Teilhard's prayer to this Christ:

> Lord of consistence and union, you whose distinguishing mark and essence is the power indefinitely to grow greater, without distortion or loss of continuity, to the measure of the mysterious Matter whose Heart you fill and all whose movements you ultimately control—Lord of my childhood and Lord of my last days—God, complete in relation to yourself and yet, for us, continually being born—God, who, because you offer yourself to our worship as 'evolver' and 'evolving,' are henceforth the only being that can satisfy us—sweep away at last the clouds that still hide you—the clouds of hostile prejudice and those, too, of false creeds.
>
> Let your universal presence spring forth in a blaze that is at once Diaphany and Fire.[20]

In his book*The Divine Milieu*, Teilhard offers a prayer that he hopes that others may find inspiring and make it their own prayer:

> Grant, O God, that when I draw near to the altar to communicate, I may henceforth discern the infinite perspectives hidden beneath the nearness and the smallness of the Host in which you are concealed.
>
> I have already accustomed myself to seeing, beneath the stillness of that piece of bread, a devouring power which, in the words of the greatest doctors of your Church, far from being consumed by me, consumes me. Give me the strength to rise above the remaining illusions which tend to make me think of your touch as circumscribed and momentary.[21]

87

In the last sentence of his prayer, Teilhard used the words *circumscribed and momentary*. He is referring to the mistaken belief, often taught to children, that, once the "bread–ness" of the Host dissolves and is digested in one's stomach (a process that takes less than ten minutes), the presence of Christ disappears. What Teilhard, St. Paul, and the doctors of the church are saying is that in consuming the host, it is the ordinary human *you* that "disappears." What happens in receiving holy communion is that you renew yourself as living as part of Christ's Body. You reaffirm your being as a "new creation." Without losing anything of the ordinary human *you*, you see yourself as part of a larger, cosmic–sized Christ. *You "disappear" into Christ.* You realize that, in Christ, you are already living in and participating in the "fullness of life" as a communally shared experience.

What Teilhard wants to emphasize is that it is not only you and I who "disappear" in this Cosmic or Universal Christ. For Teilhard, every last speck of matter "disappears" in Christ and lives also in the Eucharistic Christ. He writes,

> When, through the priest, Christ says, "This is my body," the words reach out infinitely far beyond the morsel of bread over which they are pronounced: they bring the entire mystical body into being. The priestly act extends beyond the transubstantiated Host to the cosmos itself.[22]

Jesus celebrated the first Eucharist on a table in the Upper Room. Today, believers celebrate Eucharist on a marble altar in a church building.

In a mystical experience he had, Teilhard realized that the Eucharist can also be celebrated cosmically using the surface of the planet as the liturgical altar on which to pronounce the words of consecration. In this setting, saying "This is my body" refers to all of us on Earth as the Body of Christ.

Teilhard describes this wondrous experience as his Mass on the World.

5

Teilhard's Mass on the World

IN HIS DAILY journal, Teilhard recounts a powerful mystical experience he had one morning working as a geologist in the Ordos Desert of China. He called this inspired happening his "Mass on the World."[1] The event occurred shortly after sunrise in the year 1923 on the Feast of Our Lord's Transfiguration, one of Teilhard's favorite days in the liturgical calendar. His divine encounter on this day was transfigurational in itself. The experience prefigured much of the theology and spirituality developed in his book *The Divine Milieu*, written some years later.

As a Jesuit priest, Teilhard was accustomed to celebrating a traditional Latin Mass each day before breakfast. In those days, the Eucharist was always celebrated first thing in the morning, since Catholics, including priests, were not allowed to eat or drink anything before receiving holy communion.

However, on this morning, alone in this vast wasteland, Teilhard had neither the required eucharistic bread nor any wine with which to carry out the ritual. So, he was inspired to say to God, "I, your priest, will make the whole earth my altar and on it I will offer you all the labors and sufferings of the world."[2]

What Teilhard was inspired to do also happens to be a way for you and me to celebrate a spiritual Eucharist whenever and wherever we wish, especially in our hearts.

Important Teilhardian Definitions

In *The Divine Milieu*, Teilhard divides all human experiences into two categories, which he named *activities* and *passivities*.[3]

Activities include all our *freely chosen actions and decisions*; all the things that we *choose* to make happen. In his desert liturgy, Teilhard refers to these freely chosen expenditures of energy as our *human effort*.

Passivities include *what we must endure*; all the things that happen to us *unchosen*, such as pain, failure, rejection, losses, delays, missed opportunities, sickness, inclement weather, and traffic congestion. In his desert liturgy, Teilhard refers to these unwelcome expenditures of energy as our *human sufferings*.

Thus, human effort (activities) and human suffering (passivities) summarize the entire human experience. Activities are what we do; passivities include everything that is done to us. Thus, Teilhard brings the entire human experience into his liturgy.

Mass Structure

Teilhard's Mass on the World follows the basic structure of a eucharistic liturgy and contains most of the essentials. He bypasses Scripture readings and a homily, since he is alone in the quiet desert at this early hour. But he provides an Offertory, Consecration, Communion, and a Closing Prayer.

THE OFFERTORY

Since Teilhard has no bread for his Eucharist, he substitutes what bread symbolizes for him, something that nourishes and grows humanity, namely, *human effort*. Human life is nurtured and developed by our physical labor, study, research, all forms of work and striving. The "bread" he lifts up to God at the offertory includes all the effort and labor "that men and women will perform this day all over the world." For Teilhard, this "bread" contains every effort (*activity of growth*) that helps to keep evolution moving forward and upward toward greater consciousness of our human purpose on Earth.

Teilhard's Mass on the World

Since Teilhard has no wine for his Eucharist, he substitutes what wine symbolizes for him, something that must be crushed, like grapes, before they become wine. For him, wine represents whatever crushes the efforts of humanity. His symbolic wine includes all the suffering people will undergo that day. This includes energy expended enduring pain, anguish, frustrations, confusions, failures, losses, and death — whatever, that day, will hinder and diminish human striving and frustrate the ongoing work of men and women (*passivities of diminishment*).

So, in his offering of all that day's *human effort* and *human suffering*, Teilhard presents to God the totality of human life and experience that will happen to the human family. The offering contains all the combined efforts and work of the human race (the bread) as well as all the energy to be spent enduring the suffering and diminishments of the human race (the wine).

At his Mass on the World, Teilhard also has a *congregation*. He is not celebrating a liturgy in private, though it may look like that to someone observing him. He is envisioning *all humanity as his congregation*. In Teilhard's own words,

> I call before me the whole vast anonymous army of living humanity; those who surround me and support me though I do not know them; those who come, and those who go; above all, those who in office, laboratory and factory,...truly believe in the progress of earthly reality and who today will take up again their impassioned pursuit of the light.

The *altar* on which Teilhard presents his offering to God is the entire planet. *Earth itself is the only table big enough to serve as his altar.* On this planetary altar he places the offerings of all humanity, the bread of all our activities of growth and the wine of all our passivities of diminishment.

This is a liturgy celebrated on the altar of the world by everyone living this day on our planet Earth. They are not only the *congregation*, they are also the *offering*.[4] Through Teilhard's priestly hands, he lifts up as an offering to God all humanity's efforts and all its suffering.

Teilhard suggests that this is what you and I are meant to bring to the offertory at each eucharistic liturgy we attend — to put our day's efforts into the bread on the altar and our day's suffering and diminishments into the cup of wine. More accurately, we are to put into our offering all the efforts plus all the suffering of *everyone* in the congregation. At any liturgy, Teilhard wants us consciously to connect with the *whole worshiping body*, not to think merely of our individual selves.

THE CONSECRATION

After the Offertory comes the Eucharistic Prayer and the Consecration. At the beginning of each Eucharistic Prayer, the priest asks God's Holy Spirit to come and transform the bread and wine into the body and blood of Christ. In Teilhard's Mass on the World, he asks God's Spirit to come and transform what is being offered on the altar of the world into the living Christ. Teilhard cries out to the Holy Spirit,

> Blazing Spirit, Fire,...be pleased yet once again to come down and breathe a soul into the newly formed, fragile film of matter with which this day the world is to be freshly clothed.

First, to transform his symbolic bread (our activity and effort), Teilhard asks God's Spirit—the divine Fire—to turn all human work and effort that will be expended on Earth today into the work and effort of the Universal Body of Christ.

Next, to transform his symbolic wine (the energy we spend suffering), Teilhard also asks God's Spirit to turn all human diminishment—the blood, sweat, and tears that will be shed on Earth today—into the suffering of the Universal Body of Christ. This self–offering is what St. Paul meant when he said, "In my flesh I am completing what is lacking in Christ's afflictions" (Col 1:24).

Teilhard then speaks the words of consecration, "*This is my body....This is my blood.*" And in that moment, he professes his belief that this transformation of human effort and suffering is truly happening, that what he and we are offering is acceptable to God. He trusts that this ritual action is somehow helping to complete the work of God, namely, the divine evolutionary Christ project that the Creator set in motion at the first moment of creation.

Of course, every morning that Teilhard was in the desert without bread or wine he could have offered this Mass on the World. And so can we, whenever the sacred liturgy in a church is unavailable. As a member of a priestly people and as a member of the Body of Christ, each of us can spiritually celebrate a Mass on the World every day. Each one of us can represent the human race—as well as the Body of Christ—and offer to God not only our own personal activities and passivities but also all the collective efforts and diminishments that humanity and the Earth itself will experience this day.

The daily efforts of humanity (each one's activities of growth) somehow help enrich the Universal Christ. Each day, we can also redirect the energy we spend suffering (our passivities of diminishment) to help move Christ one inch forward and upward toward his completion and fulfillment.

A Shift in Understanding

For Teilhard, at the consecration of the world as described in his Mass on the World—as well as at the consecration in the Eucharist at daily liturgy—the Holy Spirit is transforming the bread and wine not merely into the body and blood of Jesus of Nazareth, but more fully into the cosmic being that is the Universal Christ that lives today. In Teilhard's words, "In the new humanity which is begotten today the divine Word prolongs the unending act of his own birth." For Teilhard, the incarnation will not be complete until every particle of the universe becomes fully alive in Christ.

In other words, what is consecrated today is Christ. What is consecrated tomorrow will be the same Christ. Yet somehow, tomorrow at the consecration, Christ in his Body will have grown because of our efforts and our sufferings today. We strive to transform our lives and the world itself in Christ today, so that the Universal Christ tomorrow may become a bit more manifest to the world than he is today.

THE COMMUNION

In his Mass on the World, as Teilhard accepts this spiritual communion, he pictures taking into himself the Fire of the Holy Spirit.

In its true meaning, communion involves not merely eating together but, more properly, bringing about a spiritual and physical union of hearts and bodies of the worshipers gathered in this place. Teilhard also sees the moment of communion as a time when each one reaffirms his or her part in humanity's covenant with God. Teilhard clearly accepts his personal role and responsibility in this divine process: "If the Fire has come down into the heart of the world it is, in the last resort, to lay hold on me and to absorb me."

Teilhard's communion is not only a communion between him and Christ, but also a communion with all worshipers. In his communion, he agrees to fulfill his own part in the Body of Christ's task of creating a loving union of all that exists. What Teilhard takes responsibility for is fostering the continued health and growth the Universal Christ, since in Christ, at this moment and in every moment, we live and move and have our being.

At the end of time, there will be one Body and one Spirit in love with itself and with all the individuals in it.

We too can envision each of our own communions as a way of uniting ourselves with the efforts and desires of the Great Christ. We can say with Teilhard, "Lord Jesus,…beneath those world–forces you have become truly and physically everything for me, everything about me, everything within me." Communion is not simply a spiritual event; it also has its physical and organic dimensions.

When we take communion during a liturgical celebration, the small element of the sacred species changes us and transforms us over time, little by little, into Christ. Likewise, in this spiritual Eucharist, as we align ourselves with the efforts and desires of the Great Christ, it transforms us little by little so that his heart's desire becomes our heart's desire.

THE CLOSING PRAYER

In our daily eucharistic service, the liturgy closes with a final prayer. So does Teilhard's Mass on the World. His prayer is much longer than a usual liturgical Postcommunion Prayer. He begins by praying for what this grand communion means to him personally:

Lord Jesus, beneath those world–forces you have become truly and physically everything for me, everything about me, everything within me. Now, I shall gather into a single prayer both my delight in what I have and my thirst for what I lack.

Nothing, Lord Jesus, can subsist outside of your flesh; so that even those who have been cast out from your love are still, unhappily for them, the beneficiaries of your presence upholding them in existence. All of us, inescapably, exist in you, the universal *milieu* in which and through which all things live and have their being.

For Teilhard, there is nothing outside the Christ. Teilhard summarizes his vision:

For me, my God, all joy and all achievement, the very purpose of my being and all my love of life, all depend on this one basic vision of the union between yourself and the universe.

Your Mass on the World

If you wish, whenever you have no access to a normal liturgical service in a church, you can celebrate a Mass on the World as a personal devotion. Use your imagination to help visualize the process. Follow the same five steps as Teilhard's Mass on the World — Offertory, Eucharistic Prayer, Consecration, Communion, and Closing Prayer.

Your Offertory. The altar may begin in your room, but imagine its surface stretching out all over city and state and even over the whole world.

For the bread, you can use your imagination to picture all the thousands of ways people today are striving to make their world a better place, including your own efforts. You may envision some people laboring, others studying, teams researching, groups meeting, some praying, some playing, others teaching, serving, counseling, caring, healing, and so on. These activities of growth form the bread you place on your altar.

For the wine, use your imagination to picture all the thousands of ways people today, including you, are undergoing unavoidable suffering — loss of job, frustration, sickness, poverty, hunger, cold, failure, pain, separation, death, and all the rest of the diminishments humans suffer. The energy spent enduring these passivities of diminishment produces the wine you place on the altar.

Your Eucharistic Prayer and Consecration. In your own words, express your belief that the Holy Spirit is transforming these gifts —

which in fact include you—into the Great Body of Christ. Pray that you and the rest of humanity today will in some little way help the Cosmic Christ take one small step toward its fulfillment—the *Pleroma* of St. Paul and the Omega Point of Teilhard.

Focused on the offerings on your altar of the world, unite your priestly heart together with everyone on the altar. On behalf of all, ask God's Holy Spirit to transform these offerings into the body and lifeblood of the Universal Christ who lives today. In your heart—and living in the Body of Christ—say, *"This is my body....This is my blood."*

Your Communion. With Teilhard, you and all of us welcome into our hearts the life of the Great Christ, the breath and blood of this Christ, asking him to transform our consciousness and us. Invite the Universal Christ to transform our hearts, so that Christ's heart's desire becomes everyone's heart's desire. Promise to accept your responsibilities in furthering the growth of the Body of Christ in every way you can.

Your Closing Prayer. In Teilhard's words,

> For me, my God, all joy and all achievement, the very purpose of my being and all my love of life, all depend on this one basic vision of the union between yourself and the universe. AMEN! Thank You!

The Image of Fire

In his Mass on the World, Teilhard often used images of fire and flames. He viewed fire symbolically, both as the Fire of the Holy Spirit and as the symbol of desire that enflames the Heart of Christ. Teilhard was very deeply devoted to the Sacred Heart of Christ. It was a devotion he learned at an early age from his mother. It remained central to his spiritual life and his spiritual practices. The image of fire in Teilhard's thought is more fully developed in the following chapter.

6

The Heart of Christ

From the Heart of Jesus to the Heart of Christ

TEILHARD'S MOTHER awakened in him a devout passion for spiritual experience when she taught him childhood prayers, especially devotion to the Sacred Heart of Jesus. The young Pierre would stare reverently at the family's large statue of the Sacred Heart and focus on the metal rays emanating outward from the heart of Jesus. This childhood longing to know God would evolve into a most creative eucharistic mysticism.

Teilhard's devotion to the Sacred Heart became the foundation of his cosmic vision of Christ and the Eucharist. His spiritual practice evolved from a focus on the Sacred Heart of Jesus of Nazareth into a focus on the Heart of the Universal Christ.

Teilhard's prayer to the Sacred Heart of *Christ* differed greatly from the traditional devotion to the Sacred Heart of *Jesus* that burst forth in France during the time of Louis XIV in the eighteenth century and continued well into the twentieth.

The traditional form of Sacred Heart devotion had four characteristics. First, its purpose was almost exclusively focused on making "reparation for sin." Second, Teilhard noted that, in paintings and statues, "the heart of our Savior [was] depicted with curiously anatomical realism."[1] Third, the traditional devotion envisioned Christ no further than Jesus of Nazareth suffering and dying on the cross; it did not include the resurrected Christ or the Universal Body of Christ. Fourth, it promoted a spirituality that stressed rejection of the world.[2] This narrow view in devotional prayers to the Sacred Heart can still be seen today.

Teilhard was never attracted to these aspects of the devotion. "What attracted him to the Sacred Heart was its symbolic power and its superhuman appeal....The Sacred Heart...was for Teilhard a means of devotional escape from whatever was 'too narrow, too precise, and too limited' in the traditional image of Christ."[3] Teilhard wrote,

> I was still not yet in my theological studies when through and under the symbol of the Sacred Heart, the Divine had already taken on for me the form, the consistence and properties of an ENERGY, of a FIRE. By that I mean that it had become able to insinuate itself everywhere, to be metamorphosed into no matter what. And so, in as much as it was patient of being universalized, it could in future force its way into, and so amorize, the cosmic Milieu.[4]

Amorize is a neologism of Teilhard. It means "to fill with love" or "to transform through love." The image of Christ's Cosmic Heart continued to be a focal point of his spirituality. To the very end of his life, Teilhard kept on his writing desk an icon of the radiant Heart of Christ.

At the same time as his spiritual life was growing deeper, Teilhard was discovering "another half of myself," his love of matter. This was manifested in his geological explorations, a scientific field that fascinated him and in which he would make his "home" for the rest of his life.

Traditionally, the church warned us that we should be wary of the world, as it was a place of trials, tribulations, and sin. Familiar prayers to Our Lady and to Jesus reminded us that on Earth, we are "exiles." We live in a "valley of tears." Even in some of today's liturgical prayers, we are encouraged to see ourselves as "in the world, but not *of* it."

Recently, in a total reversal of this traditional perception, Pope Francis has called Earth "our home."[5] On Earth is where the kingdom of God is actively at work today. God's presence among us in the "world" is a primary message of Jesus (Matt 4:17).

Through the Sacred Heart of Christ, Teilhard was able to begin joining together the two loves of his own heart: spirit and matter. As Teilhard explained, "My progress in this direction was made easier by the fact that 'my mother's God' was primarily, for me as well as for her, the *incarnate* Word."[6] To "incarnate" describes the act of a purely spiritual being taking on or assuming a life of flesh and blood; a process of divine enfleshment; an intimate union of spirit and matter.

The integration of matter and spirit in Jesus provided for Teilhard the first connection between the spiritual and the material. In the Sacred Heart that he envisioned, the Divine Spirit joined itself not merely to the human body of Jesus of Nazareth, but to all matter. Christ's Cosmic Heart continues to give divine life to the entire universe. In his personal journal Teilhard wrote, "The Sacred Heart is the Center of Christ who centers all on himself." For Teilhard, "all" refers to the entire universe.

Teilhard raised the image of the Sacred Heart to cosmic dimensions. In his vision, the evolution and fulfillment of the universe was wedded to the fulfillment of Christ and his universal Body. Teilhard might express this union by saying that cosmogenesis (the becoming and development of the universe) and Christogenesis (the becoming and development of the universal Body of Christ) were happening simultaneously. As a scientist, Teilhard saw the evolution of the universe as cosmogenesis. As a theologian, he saw it as Christogenesis. Both processes had the same heart. In his personal journal he wrote, "Heart of Jesus, Heart of Evolution."

Although the early church was not familiar with the concept of evolution, the cosmic dimension of Christ was part of early Christianity. For example, St. Athanasius (296–373) wrote, "God was consistent in working through one man to reveal himself everywhere, as well as through the other parts of his creation, so that nothing was left devoid of his divinity and his self–knowledge...so that the whole universe was filled with the knowledge of the Lord as the waters fill the sea."[7] Personal attachment to the Heart of Christ became the seed of Teilhard's Christology, which, in turn, formed the most substantial part of his religious thought, including his cosmic understanding of the Eucharist.

The Sacred Heart as Universal

Teilhard developed a positive and forward–looking devotion to the Sacred Heart. He rescued it from sentimentality and superstition and integrated it into his vision of the evolving universe. He describes his vision of the Sacred Heart sublimely in *The Heart of Matter*. Robert Speaight, a Teilhard biographer, summarized this mystical event:

> Teilhard [in his early twenties] recalls an evening when he had spoken of his vision of Christ, of how the universe had come to assume for him the lineaments of the divine figure. Pausing one day before the image of the Sacred Heart, he had wondered how an artist might possibly represent the humanity of Jesus without giving it a beauty too individual and exclusive.[8]

And then the mystical vision began.

> Gradually the contours of the picture—the folds of the robe, the radiance of the head—dissolved without quite disappearing, so that on the surface of separation between Christ and the world the limits of either became indistinguishable. The vibration extended to the limits of the universe itself, but when the objects included in it were examined one by one they still preserved their individual character. They were transformed, but they were not lost; leading the gaze of the beholder back to the source of their illumination which was the face of Christ himself.[9]

Moreover, in the image–experience described above, that Cosmic Heart "brought the transfiguration (or transmutation) of the Corporeal into an incredible Energy of Radiation."[10] The fire in that Cosmic Heart *changed matter into energy.*[11]

Teilhard tried to explain the transformation that was happening in the image of the Sacred Heart as he gazed at it:

> But there came a second stage when this [human–divine thing] lit up and exploded from within. There was no longer a patch of crimson in the center of Jesus, but a glowing core of fire, whose splendor embraced every contour—first those of the God–Man—and then those of all things that lay within his ambience.[12]

100

The Divine was joining itself to Matter, to all the Human, in the direction of the infinity of the ages lying ahead.[13]

In traditional spirituality, the Sacred Heart of Jesus was a human heart pumping within the chest of a human being. As a human heart, it weighed, at most, a few pounds. In Teilhard's Sacred Heart of Christ, he saw an immense human–divine heart at the center of the cosmos pumping love and life into everything in the universe.

Sacred Heart as Fire at the Center of the Universe

In a series of images in various writings, Teilhard explained how prayer to the Sacred Heart of the cosmos enriched his understanding of Christ. For example, he says, this devotion gave him "a sense of the solidity of Christ...the immersion of the divine in the corporeal...a glowing core of fire...able to insinuate itself everywhere...making love the energy of the cosmic milieu." The Sacred Heart of Christ provided the "alchemical vessel in which fiery transformation happens."

Traditional Sacred Heart devotion focused on the human heart of Jesus of Nazareth. But for Teilhard, the Sacred Heart of Christ was no longer merely the heart of the individual Jesus of Nazareth. It became the true heart of each person and being in the Body of Christ. The Heart of Christ represented "the immersion of the Divine in the Corporeal." For Teilhard, the Heart of Christ revealed itself as the heart of the cosmos. It pulsed life into everyone and every individual thing. It was the heart of everything, even of every atomic particle.

Teilhard used the image of the Sacred Heart to develop his vision of Christ's fire radiating from the center of the universe:

Christ, his heart a fire, capable of penetrating everywhere, and gradually spreading everywhere....Our spiritual being is continually nourished by the countless energies of the tangible world."[14]

However, in this second stage of the image–vision, the change from matter into energy, Teilhard wrote, "My mother's Christ was somehow

101

'de–individualized' for me into a form that was 'substantially' hardly representational." There was no way this transfiguration could be captured in a drawing.

Deindividualizing the Sacred Heart[15]

When Scripture says, "Our God is a consuming fire" (Heb 12:29), fire may also be understood as a metaphor for the burning up (consuming) of ego–centeredness. For most of us, our lives are centered around what our ego wants—attention, admiration, comfort, security, pleasure, and self–focus. Ego–centeredness says, "*My* will be done," in contrast to the Lord's Prayer's, "*Thy* will be done." When you enter deeply into life in the eucharistic Christ, you become part of a human–divine Being that is higher and greater than yourself.

Once you experience the freedom of living this larger life in Christ, you wish only to carry out the work of Christ on Earth. Living in the eucharistic Christ, even while remaining an individual human being, you learn to let go of your sense of living merely an individual life. Connected to all the others in Christ, you belong to a much greater organism doing Christ's work on Earth.

By picturing the Heart of Christ as *Fire*, we can invite Christ's Fire to both consume our self–centeredness and enflame our hearts, so that we share the Fire that would transform the world. In that alchemical blaze, one's human ego values are transformed from the baser metals of self–concern and self–centeredness into the gold of humility and generosity. In our spiritual practice, we learn to turn our ego energy into compassion for others, not at the cost of personal esteem but as a fruit of it.

When Christ's Heart becomes your life's center, you realize that Christ's Heart wishes to become the fiery center of every heart for all time.

This prayer of St. Margaret Mary states the connection well:

O divine fire...consume me and I will not resist....Your lively flames make those live who die in them....I adore you most Sacred Heart of Jesus. Inflame my heart with the divine love with which your own is all on fire.

In traditional spirituality, fire is often associated with punishment of the damned. But in the context of revelations from the mystics, *fire is about love.* The Sacred Heart's Fire is a divine pledge that the world will not end by fire but *be reborn in it.* Christ. Fire was Teilhard's luminous metaphor of the Sacred Heart of Christ in the universe.

Teilhard sees divine consciousness as the deepest "within" of all things, the ultimate interior reality of each of us and of all creation. As we experience this divine immanence and are reborn in it, it urges us to move toward more and more transcendence. The Sacred Heart reveals that the center of God is love and that our soul's center is love too, if only we allow the divine Fire to release it. For Teilhard, *divine love is the Fire driving evolution.* He writes, "We are evolution looking at itself and conscious of itself." With the advent of humanity, consciousness becomes reflectively aware of itself for the first time. The emergence on Earth of consciousness is as big an event as the emergence of the first atom almost 14 billion years ago. With human self–reflective consciousness, evolution is heading toward ever–deepening centeredness in Christ. Teilhard used the luminous metaphor of Fire to describe how the Sacred Heart of Christ works in the universe.

The Sacred Heart and Omega

For Teilhard, Omega—the complete fulfillment of the kingdom of God in the universe—is neither abstract nor hypothetical, but a living reality ahead of us calling us to grow toward it.[16] Omega, as the *Christ who will be,* describes a future Heart of Christ that is already present, actively suffusing and permeating the Earth with its telluric energy. "I probably would never have dared to consider or form the rational hypothesis of it," Teilhard writes, "if I had not already found in my consciousness as a believer not only the speculative model for it, but its living reality."[17]

This "living reality" is, of course, the radiant Heart of Christ, which Teilhard first met as a child and which continued to grow in him throughout his life as a palpably real and personal presence. He came to see that not only his own heart but also all the hearts of the entire planet were increasingly enfolded within the immediately experiential realm of "the Christic."

The Sacred Heart on Faith and Suffering

From the center of Christ's heart, divine energy pulsates out in radiant waves, serenely carrying the world toward its consummation in Omega.

Teilhard had a *felt–sense* conviction of the presence of Christ already at work in "the stuff of the universe," directing the course of evolution from within Earth's planetary marrow. At the same time, the Sacred Heart became for him a model for dealing with the unavoidable pain and suffering of life (passivities of diminishment).

This conviction allowed him over a lifetime of otherwise unbearable diminishments to "stay the course." Teilhard personally bore untold personal suffering—chronic physical illness, emotional alienation from his fellow Jesuits, intellectual denial by church authorities, and spiritual abandonment. But he endured them all because he could see a world that was already luminously inhabited by Christ. He had learned to see in ways that others could not see.

Teilhard offers a searing meditation on the uncertainty of human success and nature's evident lack of interest concerning human efforts to improve the conditions of life. Just as Christ suffered and died in an effort to change the world, so humans living in Christ today (like Teilhard) expend immense energy trying to change a world that is apparently unresponsive to human suffering:

Ah, you know it yourself, Lord, through having borne the anguish of it as a man: on certain days the world seems a terrifying thing: huge, blind, and brutal. It buffets us about, drags us along, and kills us with complete indifference. Heroically, it may truly be said, humans have contrived to create a more or less habitable zone of light and warmth in the midst of the cold, dark waters—a zone where people have eyes to see, hands to help, and hearts to love. But how precarious that habitation is! At any moment the vast and horrible thing may break in through the cracks—the thing we try hard to forget is always there, separated from us by a flimsy partition: fire, pestilence, storms, earthquakes. Or the unleashing of dark moral forces—these callously sweep

104

away in one moment what we have laboriously built up and beautified with all our intelligence and all our love.[18]

This lamentation is merely the first paragraph of a longer passage. Accepting his responsibility as an adult in the Universal Christ, Teilhard immediately offers his response—quintessentially Teilhardian. He takes refuge in that intimate yet cosmic–sized eucharistic Heart of Christ, sensed through the eyes of faith:

> Since my dignity as a man [an adult], O God, forbids me to close my eyes to this—as an animal or a child might—that I may not succumb to the temptation to curse the universe and him who made it, teach me to adore it by seeing you concealed within it. O Lord, repeat to me the great liberating words, the words which at once reveal and operate: *Hoc est corpus meum* ["This is my body"]. In truth, the huge and dark thing, the phantom, the storm—if we want it to be so, is you! *Ego sum, nolite timere* ["It is I; do not be afraid"]. The things in our life that terrify us, the things which threw you yourself into agony in the garden, are, ultimately, only the species or appearance, the matter of one and the same sacrament.[19]

This is Teilhard's faith statement. Notice, however, that for him faith is not primarily a matter of assent to a rationally derived set of doctrines and principles.[20] Faith is first and foremost an *action*—an "operative" as he calls it. Devotion to the Heart of Christ was for him a firm commitment to social and evolutionary change. With this devotion—through the radiance of his vision of the Sacred Heart as Fire—Teilhard could look squarely in the face of suffering, reversal, and evil.

Some believers try to live their faith from the "top down," by first convincing themselves of the logical plausibility of doctrines and dogmas. Teilhard begins from the "bottom up," *by acting in alignment with* his faith. Then, he waits to see what happens next! Faith, for Teilhard, is not some thing that we *have* or a statement we *profess*, but an *energy* we expend. Faith is the capacity for loving action.

In his prophetic vision, Teilhard could see the eventual integration of matter and spirit:

Matter is the matrix of Spirit. Spirit is the higher state of Matter. These two propositions became the real axis of my inner vision and progress, and in them the word *spirit* was henceforth to bear a precise and concrete meaning. Spirit has become *the clearly defined term of a defined operation.*[21]

For Teilhard, Christ's eucharistic heart was carrying out a *divinely defined operation* with a *clearly defined divine term* of completion. Today, Christ's eucharistic Heart is still a Heart on Fire with a divine love that wants to transform the world, not only its mental and spiritual layers, but also its deepest layers of matter.

The Word of God became incarnate in the physical body of Jesus of Nazareth. The Heart of Christ wants to extend the incarnation into every particle of the universe. It is a Heart on Fire "with the power to penetrate all things—and which is now gradually spreading unchecked."[22]

Looking Ahead

Part 1 of this book presents the *intellectual* content for a basic understanding of Teilhard's theology of Christ and the Eucharist, more specifically of "Christ *in* the Eucharist." Part 2 offers some ways to *experience* Christ in the Eucharist as Teilhard might have experienced them. The spiritual practices in part 2 are designed to help others learn to "see" and "act" the way he might have seen and acted. Hopefully, they offer some fresh and revelatory ways of relating to the Eucharistic Christ.

Here is a foretaste of contemplative suggestions that are in part 2.

If you are at a liturgy, during the consecration use your imagination to picture a mist of Christ's love energy bursting from the host and cup, visibly saturating the entire church building so that each person in the congregation is inhaling Christ's love energy with each breath. Look around at people and visualize them inhaling this heavenly atmosphere.

II

CONTEMPLATIVE
SUGGESTIONS

Introduction

The Eucharist:
Teilhard's Favorite Subject of Prayer

AFTER TEILHARD'S death, Henri de Lubac, fellow Jesuit and
longtime friend, had access to Teilhard's meditation notebooks.
After reading them, Fr. de Lubac reported that "it was perhaps in the
mystery of his Eucharist that Jesus Christ was most often the subject"
of Teilhard's personal meditative prayer.[1]

Since Teilhard's theology of the Eucharist and of the Universal
Christ both come from his prayerful reflections, it seems most appropriate to offer some contemplative suggestions in the second part of
this book.

From Teilhard's Ten Basic Premises and his Ten Eucharistic
Premises, it is safe to say that *he viewed the universe as an extension of
the Eucharist*. He wrote, "In an extended yet real sense, the total Host
is the universe which Christ penetrates and vivifies."[2]

Exploring Teilhard's way of praying to — and in — the "total Host"
is the twofold purpose of part 2: First, to help people become familiar with praying from within the *collective* Body of Christ. Second, to
begin praying, as Teilhard might say, *evolutely*. Together, these two
approaches to prayer help integrate evolutionary processes into one's
perception of God's activity in the world.

Teilhard had no intention of starting a new school of spirituality. As a Jesuit, he was always Ignatian in his prayer. His contribution
reminded people of faith that God's work of transforming the world in
love is essentially a project that is both *collective* and *evolutionary*.

First, the work of God on Earth and in heaven gets done *collectively*. It is accomplished primarily through *collaborative efforts* of

groups of people—bodies, minds, and hearts—committed to a shared loving purpose. Even Jesus needed a team working with him in Galilee and Judea.

Second, Teilhard showed how the kingdom of God and the (Mystical) Body of Christ are continually *evolving*, that is, reaching new levels of complexity, consciousness, and love.

Jesus taught that the work of God's kingdom was active on Earth here and now. As members of the universal Body of Christ, says St. Paul, we are his arms, legs, eyes, ears, mouth, and voice working and praying *together* to keep his Body *evolving* here and now.

For most of us, to look at the host and see Christ holding the entire evolving universe in his hands, will require "new eyes." To pray like Teilhard, we will need to evolve in faith into new ways of seeing reality.

As humans, we are hardwired to evolve new eyes to observe what God is doing all around us. But it takes practice—like learning to play a musical instrument—to develop our ability to use these new eyes in our daily life.

Learning to See with New Eyes

Early in the twentieth century, few people, including church officials, could imagine how an understanding of evolution could foster a deeper and richer understanding of the Eucharist. With his ability to think *evolutely*, Teilhard could see what others could not see. He practiced continually using his new eyes. He recognized evolution's value in enriching our understanding of Christ, and he saw its potential decades before any other Christian theologian or scientist. He wanted to teach people to see the Eucharist in ways he could see it. Like a dedicated and patient music teacher, he viewed his mission on Earth as helping us develop skill in using our new eyes for this purpose.

In the introduction to his book on spirituality, *The Divine Milieu*, Teilhard explicitly stated this purpose. His desire was to teach people "how to see God everywhere, to see him in all that is most hidden, most solid, and most ultimate in the world."[3] He wanted God to "become for you [and me] universally perceptible and active—very near and very distant at one and the same time."[4]

110

Introduction

With the boldness of a mystic, Teilhard enthusiastically showed us how to put on the mind of Christ, to see things with the eyes of the Universal Christ. Instead of just seeing Jesus of Nazareth (the Christ who was) in the Eucharist, Teilhard wanted to show us how to see in the host the Christ who is today and the Christ who will be.

In gospel stories, Jesus invites us to enter the kingdom of God. He wants us to be able to recognize divine activity at work everywhere. But before we can recognize the workings of the kingdom all around us, Jesus is clear about what is needed. He says that we need to undergo a *metanoia*. "From that time Jesus began to proclaim, 'Repent [undergo *metanoia*], for the kingdom of heaven has come near'" (Matt 4:17).

Metanoia is a Greek word, used by both John the Baptist and Jesus (see Matt 3:2 and 4:17). It means to adopt a higher (*meta*) mind-set (*noia*), that is, a more open and perceptive way of thinking and perceiving.[5] In other words, to put on new eyes.

Only by developing a higher level of consciousness—and "new eyes"—will we be able to see creation the way Jesus and the Baptist saw it. In one of Jesus's sayings recorded in the Gospel of Thomas, Jesus tells his disciples that, if they want to step into the kingdom of God and observe it at work everywhere, they need to replace their normal eyes with new eyes:

> When you are able to fashion an eye to replace an eye, and form a hand in place of a hand, or a foot for a foot, making one image supercede another—then you will enter in.[6]

Again, in Teilhard's major scientific book on the evolution of the universe, *The Human Phenomenon*, he stressed to his readers the importance of learning to see things in this new way. He felt that "new eyes" were needed for someone that wanted to see creation evolutely as he could. In *Phenomenon*'s prologue he wrote,

> *Seeing.* One could say that the whole of life lies in seeing—if not ultimately, at least essentially. To become more is to become more united….But unity grows…only if it is supported by an increase of consciousness, of vision. This is probably why the history of the living world can be reduced to the elaboration of ever more perfect eyes at the heart of a cosmos where it is always possible to discern more.[7]

Teilhard de Chardin on the Eucharist

For Teilhard, every endeavor begins with *seeing*. In our ordinary lives, the ability to visualize the structure, outcome, and effects of a project is a most essential first step in starting any process. As we learn to perceive God's project more clearly and from a wider perspective, it enables richer knowing, deeper loving, and closer following of Christ.

For example, when we look at the sacred host and chalice at Mass, Teilhard wants us to learn to see the whole Christ there—not just Jesus of Nazareth. For the most part, our liturgy and Bible study emphasize the life and teachings of Jesus of Nazareth, which is a good beginning. But, when Christ is studied exclusively as Jesus of Nazareth, it could keep us from getting to know the risen Christ as St. Paul and St. John deeply knew him.

To Paul and John, the resurrected Jesus Christ became, so to speak, reincarnated in a totally new way. He took on, as it were, a "third nature"—a *cosmic nature*—that was different from either his *human nature* or his *divine nature*. The glorified physical Body that the resurrected Lord entered was not merely the body of a single human being. His new "Body" was the whole of creation—including all the natural world as well as us humans. The universe lived—and continues to live—within Christ's cosmic nature.

Also, each day at the eucharistic liturgy, Jesus Christ is, so to speak, reincarnated in another totally new way. He takes on, as it were, a "fourth nature"—a *eucharistic nature*—which is different from the other three. In the Eucharist, the physical "body" that Christ enters is not the body of a single human being (Jesus of Nazareth) nor the body of the whole creation (Cosmic Christ). The "body" into which he incarnates in the liturgy each day is a small piece of bread and a cup of wine (the Eucharistic Christ). No matter the form, size, or nature of the body in which he is manifested, it is always the same Person: Christ Jesus.

Teilhard wants to show us how to refocus our eyes more discerningly on the Eucharist, and to reenvision the eucharistic presence as Christ permeating the entire universe. Teilhard saw the risen Christ operating "at the heart of a cosmos where it is always possible to discern more."

We adhere to Christ in all the ordinary actions of living. To live in the conscious awareness that we live and act in the Body of Christ, we live in a *continuous eucharistic union*. In heaven, this union will simply become a *permanent eucharistic union.*[8]

Once we can "see" in the Eucharist the whole Christ, the Universal or Cosmic Christ that lives today, it produces three changes in us. First, it reshapes what we experience on our altars and in our very beings during liturgy. Second, it expands and transforms our understanding of his awesome presence among us in daily life. Third, it previews what life will be like in heaven.

Throughout the ages, mystics, artists, and visionaries like Teilhard have been trying to get us to see what they can see that we cannot see. To explain how to open our eyes—or to put on new eyes—often requires language that is creatively unusual, fresh imagery that expresses the love of God, communion with God, even union with God.

Theologian Carl McColman makes a distinction between a saint and a mystic. "A saint is someone who is good and holy, while a mystic is someone who knows God and whose life has been transfigured by this divine presence. Put even more briefly, saints embody *goodness* while mystics embody *love*...mystics *teach* us how to find God."[9] In Richard Rohr's words, "A mystic is simply *one who has moved from mere belief or belonging systems to actual inner experience of God.*"[10]

Mystics understood a simple secret. Their secret was to use their imagination to broaden and deepen their spiritual capacities. Teilhard wants to teach you how to use your imagination to help you put on new eyes so that you can see what he sees in the Eucharist. He wants you to use your imagination to broaden and deepen your faith vision.

Imagination

Your imagination is the only faculty you have that can integrate your body, mind, and spirit and can hold in one image the past, present, and future. In your imagination you can even assemble and put together two or more things that are not in any way connected in the "real" world. Philosophers such as Aristotle and Aquinas have recognized this unique ability of the human imagination.[11]

Imagination has played a key role in the evolution of literature, poetry, drama, art, architecture, science, technology, mathematics, dreams, planning, goal setting, and all forms of creating. Some famous imaginative thinkers include Leonardo da Vinci, René Descartes, William Wordsworth, Samuel Taylor Coleridge, Albert Einstein — and every child.

> My mom watched my niece as she was intently coloring a picture. "Katie," she said, "Snowmen aren't purple." Remaining focused on her picture, Katie replied, "They are when you have an imagination."[12]

Imagination also plays a special role in the mission of a prophet. As theologian Water Brueggemans describes it,

> The prophet does not ask if the vision can be implemented, for questions of implementation are of no consequence until the vision can be imagined. The *imagination* must come before the *implementation*....It is the vocation of the prophet to keep alive the ministry of imagination, to keep on conjuring and proposing futures alternative to the single one the king [or the institution] wants to urge [upon us] as the only thinkable one.[13]

Jesus prophetically devised imaginative stories, called parables, to help explain the nature of God's kingdom. He used mustard seeds, pearls, yeast, lost coins, merchants, hidden treasure, seeds, weeds, figs, grapevines, children dancing, houses, rocks and sand, shepherds and sheep, wolves and lambs, masters and servants, and many other images to explain — and help us see — the dynamics of God's work in the world. His was a "ministry of imagination."

We learn to use imagery in our prayer life to help our eyes of faith to see more clearly.

Imagination in Spiritual Practice

Traditionally, imagination has always been a part of spiritual practices. In his *Spiritual Exercises*, the mystic St. Ignatius Loyola encourages the use of creative imagination in contemplating gospel stories to help bring these events to life.

Introduction

As a prelude to each contemplative exercise, Ignatius suggests that, by using your imagination like an artist, you can creatively paint the scene of your prayer. He calls it creating a "composition of place." Scripture seldom provides a full description of a scene. For instance, it does not provide details, such as what people look like or what they are wearing, whether they are tall or short, whether their voices are high- or low-pitched, whether they speak rapidly or slowly. And so on.

As an example, in contemplating the nativity of Jesus, Ignatius recommends that when you enter your prayer time, you are to use all the senses of your imagination to place yourself in the birth scene in great detail. He suggests using the eyes of your imagination to see details about the people and animals in the stable, the ears of your imagination to hear people's voices and the sounds of the animals, and the nose of your imagination to identify the different odors in the place. A stable would certainly produce many odors.

Ignatius asks you not only to observe the scene as a *spectator* but encourages you to place yourself in the scene as a *participant*. In this way, you can feel yourself touching things around you—noticing whether they are hard or soft, warm or cool, rough or smooth, heavy or light. He also recommends that you use your imagination to become actively engaged in the scene, perhaps by seeing yourself as a servant who brings water or a towel to Mary. In this way, Ignatius says, your contemplative experience may be deepened and enriched.

It is important to remember that imagination, by creating a vivid scene, may provide a powerful gateway to prayer and to the experience of the divine. But the "picture" is not the prayer itself. Neither is creating a detailed "picture" of the scene the purpose or goal of prayer. The real prayer is your conscious response to the presence of God.

Thomas Aquinas made the same point about imagination's power to lead us into knowledge of God's world. We begin prayer with imagination, he said, and we complete it with a conscious response to God. In Aquinas's words,

> We can use the senses and the imagination as the starting points to attain knowledge of divine things....The natural knowledge of God begins in imagination, but it ends in a prayerful act of the will, an act by which the imagined images become diaphanous or transparent, revealing their transcendent source.[14]

This is the kind of "seeing" that Teilhard is inviting us to develop—eyes that learn to see *through* the images into the divine reality that is behind them, as if the images were transparent like glass.

Imagination is one of the great gifts of God to humanity. Imagination can increase the quality of our prayer life and our active life. Imagination can help us to see everything with new eyes. These insights about imagination, Teilhard said, can "justify us in believing that we can, in strict fact, live always and everywhere without being separated from Jesus Christ."[15] Learn to use your imagination not only to intensify your prayer but also to discover God everywhere.

However, there is a stage of sharing beyond an intellectual, imagined, or even a strong affirmation of belief in the Cosmic Christ. This next stage involves building a *personal relationship* with him.

Personal Presence of Christ

There are two kinds of presence, *physical presence* and *personal presence*. People may experience physical presence without personal presence.

Personal presence is characterized by *mutual self-revelation*, that is, when each person reveals his or her thoughts and feelings while the other respectfully listens. Personal presence is typically experienced by friends, spouses, and family members. Although personal presence often involves physical presence, such sharing often transcends time and space. For example, in contemplative prayer, or in reverie where one relives a loving conversation, or more often in a phone call between friends.

Physical presence, even with an exchange of words, does not necessarily qualify as personal presence. For example, in church, saying hello or shaking hands with the person next to you is an act of connecting, but it does not qualify as mutual self-revelation. Nor does asking questions of a salesperson or thanking one for their help. Discussing details of a project with a coworker does not qualify. Probably most of our prayer time doesn't qualify as personal presence to God either. Why?

Because there is no mutual self-revelation. In your prayer, you may be sharing your feelings or making petitions to God. You may be praising God, thanking God, or expressing sorrow for your failings.

But, as such, your prayer remains a one–sided self–revelation. The words are all coming from you to God. As long as you are not listening for God's self–revelation to you, your prayer is unidirectional.

One's relationship to God—or to Christ, or to anyone else— becomes an experience of personal presence only *when you attentively listen for or observe the other's self–revelatory response.*

We all long to establish personal relationships with God the Father and with Jesus Christ. Before this can happen, we need to practice the art of personal presence by relating to the people who are near and dear to us. We begin by learning to listen attentively to the self–revelation of family members and close friends, and by responding to them with love and compassion. Attentiveness to the self–revelation of others on the human level is our preparation for being attentive to God's self–revelation.

Some people use Jesus's words found in the gospel stories as expressions of his self–revelation to them. This practice is a good start. Certain holy people that we call saints enjoyed dialogues with God. Teilhard's theology of the Eucharist and the Body of Christ, following St. Paul, offers ways to interact with the divine that invite the personal presence of mutual self–revelation.

The next time you are gazing at the Eucharist, during liturgy or in private adoration, say what you want to say to God—not too much at one time. For instance, suppose you are praying for a friend's recovery from an accident, surgery, divorce, or some loss. Make your request to God, and then remain quiet for a while. Watch what is happening in your body. Be aware if anything shifts or changes or intensifies in certain parts of your body or on your skin. Notice any images that arise spontaneously in your mind. Do any words pop into your head? Take note of them, no matter how odd they may seem at the moment.

God is not likely to strike up a conversation with you, as God apparently has done with some saints and mystics. Better to begin by exploring other ways that God and the Holy Spirit may be making their personal presence felt. Look for quiet inspirational movements happening within you. They may be physical, emotional, intellectual, or imaginal.

Since God is a God of love, you can be certain that God wishes to establish personal presence with you and in you. Unless you take the time to wait for a revelation from God during prayer, you will not learn how to be personally present to the divine.

General Suggestion for Eucharistic Prayer

As a general suggestion, when participating in the liturgy or making a personal visit to the Blessed Sacrament, instead of peppering God with a barrage of petitions and praises, try just listening. You might say to the Lord something like, "I've come to spend time with you. I won't list my petitions, since you already know them. I'm here to be in your presence. I love you." Then, just remain quiet.

You may reinforce your openness to God's personal presence by practicing it during your day. You might say, "Let me feel your presence with me as I drive to work." Or "Please accompany my children and me as we walk to the playground."

One woman keeps a painting of the Sacred Heart on her desk at work. "When I look at it," she said, "I am constantly surprised by how its quiet presence continues to call me up short. From the center of Christ's chest, it seems his energy is pulsating out in radiant waves, he seems to be serenely carrying the world forward." Her sensation that energy is emerging from within that framed image sitting on her desk is not an illusion but a way that Christ expresses his personal presence to her.

Teilhard had a *felt–sense* conviction of the presence of Christ as he carried out his geological explorations in different parts of the world. He was aware of Christ's personal presence at work in "the stuff of the universe," directing the course of evolution from within Earth's "planetary marrow." This felt awareness of Christ's self–revelation to him in "the stuff of the universe" allowed Teilhard over a lifetime of otherwise unbearable diminishments to "stay the course."

He wanted to show people how to perceive the world luminously inhabited by Christ. He wanted to explain how to learn to see Christ's Cosmic Body expressing itself—revealing itself—everywhere.

General Suggestion for Eucharistic Adoration

You are very lucky if your parish has frequent or daily exposition of the Blessed Sacrament. Compared to the normal distractions that happen during a crowded weekend liturgy in a large church, adoration in a quiet chapel provides a much more conducive atmosphere for building a deeper relationship with Christ Jesus.

Christ welcomes visitors who come just to spend time with him in the Blessed Sacrament. He is not asking you to come and recite prayers for fifteen minutes or however long you stay. Christ simply wants to be with you.

You do not have to do or say anything. If you do want to say something, just talk about what is on your mind. Not out loud, of course. Talk to him from your heart. "Lord, I'm very tired and stressed today. I hope you don't mind if I just sit here and calm down."

He is not merely your Lord and your God; he is your Brother and your Friend. You may find it easier to be personally present to him if you address him as your Brother or your Friend.

- Describe what you're preparing for dinner.
- Mention the bargain you just made at the store.
- Explain why you like a certain TV program.
- Share your plans for vacation.
- Go over some of your business projects.
- Talk about your kids or grandkids.
- Say why you enjoy talking to a certain neighbor.

Christ wants to be with you. He gives you his full attention.

St. Teresa of Avila has been named doctor of the church and is listed among the most respected authorities on prayer. Her advice to all is to think of prayer as a conversation with God. Talk to God as easily and as comfortably as you would to someone who dearly loves you. It's that simple. Think of a friend of yours—a classmate, a colleague at work, a neighbor, a relative—someone whom you love and who loves you. How do you converse with that person? How do you listen to them? That's the way to relate to God, says St. Teresa.

A Note on Doing the Right Thing

Often, at the liturgy, when the sacred host is raised immediately after consecration, people are encouraged to focus on the divinity of Christ and say in their hearts, "My Lord and my God."

During his life on Earth as Jesus of Nazareth, his apostles usually addressed him as "Master," "Teacher," or in Hebrew, "Rabbi." But Jesus called himself their Brother and Friend. He is also *your* Brother and Friend. You are Christ's brother or sister. Christ calls you *friend*. So, when you are present to the Eucharist, at the liturgy or in adoration, you may begin your prayer by addressing Christ as "My Brother and my Friend." With this attitude, you may feel it is easier to have a conversation with "someone who loves you."

In eucharistic adoration, your primary purpose is to be connected to Christ. The point is that you are *in* the host. You are already one with Christ. You are already participating in the divine mystery. Focus on being with the mystery. Don't worry about your gestures, posture, or performance, since there is no "correct" way.

For St. Paul, praying to Christ is not so much addressing someone outside us as a communion with someone inside us: "it is no longer I who live, but it is Christ who lives in me. And the life I now live in the flesh I live by faith *in the Son of God*" (Gal 2:20). For Paul and for us, both realities are true. Christ lives in us *and* we live in Christ.

Christ is walking through this cosmic mystery of transformation with us. Our job is to hold on, to remain connected and to remain in communion. When you come to spend personal time with Christ, don't get anxious about doing things right or worry about performing reverential gestures correctly. Behave in any way that feels right for you but focus on staying connected.[16] Concentrate on your loving relationship with Christ. We may think that performing ritual actions properly will make God like us better. That is impossible, since God already loves us with an infinite love.

Nevertheless, for some people reverential actions lead them to a state of awareness where they can open themselves to a deeper relationship with Christ and God. Such gestures may move them into a level of consciousness where they become more vulnerable and open to conversation with Christ. For such people, ritual movements may provide their best gateway to prayer.

St. Paul is clear. He says you don't have to act in certain ways to please God; you don't have to perform. You just need to know that you are "alive in Christ." Once you consciously accept this truth and act accordingly, the basis of your effort changes. You're not afraid of God or afraid of doing something wrong. You just want to return lovingly to the One who has always loved you.

Introduction

When you reverence Christ in the Eucharist, it is all about love, all about completing the love circuit with Christ your Brother and Friend. You look at Christ and Christ looks at you. All you need to do is receive the gaze and then return it.

With this preparation, the remainder of the book offers contemplative suggestions in the spirit of Teilhard. They are presented in two stages. Suggestions within each stage are not presented in any specific order. You may pick and choose.

Consider these suggestions as Teilhard's way of helping you acquire a new mindset and "new eyes" regarding the Eucharist. You develop your new eyes by trying new ways of praying. Give yourself permission to step into Teilhard's way of seeing Christ.

Stage One Suggestions

CONTEMPLATIVE EXERCISE 1
Seeing Rays of Divine Grace

In our church, we have a life–sized painting of Jesus Christ as Divine Mercy, reminiscent of the familiar Sacred Heart image. Most noticeable in the Divine Mercy painting are rays of grace and blessings in a variety of colors flowing from the heart of Christ. In the picture, the so–called lines of grace are strokes of color painted by an artist. They disappear into the edges of the picture frame.

However, when you are looking at the consecrated host at liturgy or during adoration of the Blessed Sacrament, those rays of blessings may be invisible, but they are very real and powerful. They are continually radiating outward from Christ's Body in the Eucharist. They don't quickly fade and disappear as they do at the edges of the painting. They keep coming from Christ toward us—and into us.

You may invite those rays of grace to be aimed and directed in many ways for your benefit as well as to enrich others. Here are a few ways to relate to Christ by directing those rays of grace and blessing.

Welcoming Eucharistic Rays. Using your imagination, picture the sacred host (or chalice) sending out rays of grace toward you. Use your imagination to help your faith visualize those rays of grace flowing from the host toward you. You may picture them having different intensities or hues. Then, let these rays be directed to those places in your body where you especially need grace or healing in your life.

For instance, suppose you must make a big decision or you're looking for some creative way to deal with a problem, imagine opening your mind and picturing rays from the host flowing through your forehead and into your brain.

If you are having trouble loving someone or need to show compassion, picture the rays of grace streaming from the host directly into your heart. If you need to show care for someone in a physical way, or your work involves your hands, open your hands toward the host and invite rays of grace from the host into your hands.

If you have arthritis in your legs, let the divine healing rays flow into the pain.

You get the idea. Wherever you need healing or support, use your imagination to direct rays of grace to that spot.

Many doctrines of our faith are difficult to understand. They may be better understood with useful imagery. For example, you may need faith to believe that divine rays of grace are entering into you. Use your imagination to support your act of faith by picturing rays of grace flowing from the host into you.

You may want to focus on the rays of grace going into your head whenever you are dealing with a decision and need God's wisdom or perspective. Or you may need to be inspired. Or you may wish to be enlightened about some Scripture passage or the meaning of an event.

If you focus on the rays of Christ flowing toward your heart, picture them opening your heart with compassion and love, or comforting your sadness or grief.

If you uncurl your fingers and let your hands face the host, picture the divine rays entering your hands, imagine how they can help you with everything you do with your hands, from hard labor to healing touch, from cooking to childcare, from sports to art to music.

You can focus Christ's rays of grace to your eyes that you may see people and events in depth, beyond what you ordinarily see.

You can focus Christ's rays of grace to your ears that you may listen and hear what is behind the words that people speak to you.

You can focus Christ's rays of grace to your mouth that you may speak with clarity and compassion to all the people you meet.

Redirecting Eucharistic Rays. To begin praying like Teilhard, refocus your attention beyond yourself by redirecting the rays of Christ's grace and love toward others.

If the person is someone presently in the church with you, you may simply ask Christ to direct special graces to that person. In your imagination, picture those rays flowing from the sacred host or cup into that person. Always add a visual image to your prayer, in order to deepen the experience and imprint it in your memory. You can carry that image with you throughout the day.

Another way to send rays of grace to a person in church is to welcome the Christ rays into yourself, and as they pass through you let them flow from you to the other person in church. They are then receiving your love as well as Christ's love. As before, always use your imagination to include a visual image—in color, if you wish—of the ray's path from the host to you and from you to the recipient.

Much in the spirit of Teilhard, a third way would be to visualize many rays of grace in a rainbow of colors flowing from the host and chalice to each person in the church. Each person lives in the Body of Christ. Those rays of grace connect us to Christ and to one another.

Another imaginative help may be for you to picture the entire congregation bathed in a holy light, spreading like an atmosphere or a mist, emanating from the Eucharist. This light does not merely surround the people. They inhale it and it enlightens each one's entire body. As you take a breath, visualize yourself inhaling air filled with the graces of the Holy Spirit. In your imagination, see your mind's images of them, as Teilhard would say, becoming "diaphanous or transparent, revealing their transcendent source."

Eucharistic Rays toward Those Not Present. Since Christ is omnipresent, his divine rays are not limited to people present in the church. You may request them to be aimed at people that are not present.

Perhaps there is someone in the hospital who is sick—or even dying. Perhaps you know a couple that are having marital problems. Or someone preparing for a big exam, or having to make an important decision, or looking for a place to live, or worried about financial matters.

Perhaps you have relatives and friends living far away that you would like to experience God's loving touch. No matter where on

Earth they may be, they too live in Christ's Body and can welcome the rays of his mercy and protection.

Christ's rays may be directed toward the poor, the outcasts, those suffering because of prejudice related to race, religion, skin color, age, or gender orientation.

Eucharistic Rays toward Nature. Since Christ holds all things in his Body in love, you may ask that his rays of love be directed to your pets or other animals. Many people are concerned with animal life and species extinction. In Florida where I live, we are concerned about wounded manatees, beached whales, and endangered species of fish. Florida is also a frequent target of hurricanes and flooding.

Whatever your concerns with nature may be, you may direct eucharistic rays to those concerns. Always remember to visualize the divine rays of your prayer.

CONTEMPLATIVE EXERCISE 2

Seeing Jesus in the Eucharist

Looking at the Host: Seeing Jesus There. The Universal or Cosmic Christ that Teilhard speaks of is always the same person as Jesus of the Gospels, except that, Jesus's time on Earth lasted about thirty–three years, while the Cosmic Christ has been growing and maturing for over two thousand years.

Nevertheless, the Cosmic Christ could not appear at the end of time unless he had inserted himself historically into the cosmos by being born of a woman as a human being.[1] So, to develop your ability to see Christ who is as Teilhard saw him, it may be best to start with Jesus of Nazareth. Begin to develop a new eucharistic spirituality by contemplating Christ in his human life living in the Holy Land. Teilhard clearly recognized the value of doing so. As he wrote in *The Divine Milieu,*

> The mystical Christ, the universal Christ of St. Paul, has neither meaning nor value in our eyes except as an explanation of the Christ who was born of Mary and who died on the cross....However far we may be drawn into the divine

126

spaces opened up to us by Christian mysticism, we never depart from the Jesus of the Gospels.[2]

St. Augustine often spoke of experiencing a eucharistic liturgy as another Nativity. Sometimes, when he lifted the sacred host after the consecration, he is said to have visualized in it the infant Jesus in Bethlehem.

As a suggestion at this early stage of putting on "new eyes," think of the Eucharist as a living photo album of Christ. By turning its pages, you and I may visualize Christ at different periods of his life — his birth, public life, death, and resurrection.

For example, I can look at a family photo album and realize that the child in the photograph is me, the teen in the photo is me, the groom in my wedding photo is me, the photo of a proud father with his daughter at her graduation is me, and the gray–haired man in the retirement photo is me. All of them are me, yet none of them is me today.

Similarly, at each liturgy when you look at the host you may use your imagination to turn the pages of Jesus's photo album and select an image for that day's contemplation.

Start by focusing on one image at a time.

Jesus's Photo Album. On one day during the liturgy, you may use your imagination to picture in the host the baby Jesus at Christmas, as St. Augustine did. At another time, it might be the twelve–year–old Jesus in the Jerusalem temple. At yet another time, you may choose to picture Jesus being baptized by John. Similarly, you may see in the host or chalice Jesus in the garden at Gethsemane, or Jesus on the cross, or the resurrected Jesus. Each of those images that you picture is true. Many saints have become saints by meditating on the mysteries of Jesus's life in Palestine.

Rather than just looking at the host, seeing bread, and making an act of faith that what you are looking at is Jesus Christ, "body and blood, soul and divinity," begin using your imagination to picture Jesus alive and active in the host. Each time you celebrate a liturgy or attend eucharistic adoration, you may envision a moving picture of a different event in Jesus's life.

You can choose an image of Jesus to fit your current situation. If you are suffering, you may picture Jesus at Gethsemane or hanging on the cross. If you are happy, perhaps choose the wedding feast at Cana. Choose a different image of Jesus depending on your present circumstances. Begin using your imagination to see him alive and active in the host.

At our church, we have eucharistic adoration each weekday. In the chapel where adoration happens, behind the monstrance are several traditional stained glass windows. From left to right: Joseph holding the child Jesus at about age one, Jesus being baptized by John, Jesus praying in agony in the garden, Jesus hanging on the cross, Jesus risen from the dead, Jesus's ascending to heaven, and Jesus revealing his Sacred Heart. I can take the stained glass images, one by one, and in my imagination, using the host like a movie screen, picture Jesus moving about at each stage of his life.

There are a number of reasons for beginning to contemplate the sacred host in this way. First, you are practicing using your imagination. Second, you are working with familiar images. Third, you can begin with any image of Jesus you wish. Fourth, if you are having difficulty with one image, you can easily switch to a different image to see if it feels more natural at the time.

Help for Getting Started. Begin simply. If you have trouble seeing Jesus active and moving or speaking to you in the host, start with just visualizing a still–life image, for instance, the baby Jesus in the manger in Bethlehem. Once you have developed that image clearly and in some detail, visualize the baby turning his head or moving an arm or curling his fingers. Next, you may visualize him whimpering or cooing.

Once you are comfortable with the baby Jesus moving, perhaps you can add Mary or Joseph into the picture. Perhaps, you can watch Mary or Joseph holding the baby closely. Eventually, you may wish to see in the host that you are holding the baby Jesus. Yes, you holding the baby Jesus.

You and I belong to Christ's Body, so we are in the host. You may picture in the nativity scene any person you wish—a child, a friend, a student. You may visualize that person holding the baby Jesus. Perhaps, you know someone who needs to feel God's love; picture that person in the host holding the baby Jesus.

The secret is to begin with the most familiar scenes of Jesus's life, scenes for which you can easily create a visual setting and envision it in the host or chalice. Some of my favorites include the following:

- Jesus at age twelve teaching the learned men in the temple
- Jesus being baptized by John in the River Jordan
- Jesus preaching in Peter's boat
- Jesus calming the stormy waters on the Sea of Galilee
- Jesus with a child seated on his lap
- Jesus healing a blind man
- Jesus sitting near the Samaritan woman at the well
- Jesus with his mother at the Cana wedding feast
- Jesus riding a donkey into Jerusalem before Passover
- Jesus at the Last Supper
- Jesus on the cross
- Jesus with Mary Magdalene near the empty tomb on Easter morning

A Larger Perspective. To understand anything or anyone fully, such as our incarnate Christ, Teilhard believes that it is not enough to focus just at the beginnings or initial stages of his development. The best grasp of someone's meaning and purpose comes from an exploration at their maturity, their fulfillment. We would not want to judge any human's life's meaning simply by his or her infancy or childhood. We would want to understand that individual by observing the length and depth of his or her entire life.[3]

Teilhard began his childhood exploration of Christ like most of us, when we were children in our mother's arms, by hearing and imagining the events of Jesus of Nazareth's life as told in the Gospels. But as we mature in our understanding, we realize that Christ's presence begins "to spread out gradually everywhere...without destroying anything that went before."

In a prayer to Christ later in his life, Teilhard describes his spiritual evolution.

> In the guise of a tiny babe in its mother's arms, obeying the great law of birth, you came, Lord Jesus, to swell in my infant soul; and then, as you re-enacted in me—and in so doing extended the range of—your growth through the Church. That same humanity which once was born and dwelt in Palestine began now to spread out gradually everywhere like an iridescence of unnumbered hues through which,

129

without destroying anything that went before, your presence penetrated—and endued with supervitality—every other presence around me.[4]

In doing these spiritual practices, you begin to understand what Teilhard meant when he experienced Christ's all–embracing presence and said to him, "Your presence penetrated…every other presence around me."

CONTEMPLATIVE EXERCISE 3
Seeing You in the Eucharist

Seeing Yourself in the Host. When gazing at the consecrated host, use your imagination to picture yourself in the host looking back at you in the pew. Let yourself realize that, in fact, you are living in Christ at this moment, even though you are kneeling in a church pew. Learn to look at your life as if you were looking at it from your place in the Body of Christ.

Perhaps, if you need to decide about some matter, you can ask the "you" in the host for some perspective on your decision. In your imagination, let the "you" in the host talk to you in the pew.

Psychologically, you might think of the "you living in the host" as your *higher self* talking to you. Having a dialogue with this higher, or transcendent, self is a way of growing in self–awareness. If you find it helpful to imagine the "you in the host" as your higher self, then you may carry on a dialogue with that higher self. You may find that such a dialogue may require a good deal of quiet time, which is not readily available during a public liturgy. Perhaps a visit to the Blessed Sacrament would be useful in such a case.

Seeing yourself in the host is a good practice to remind you that you are always being held safely in the Body of Christ.

If you are praying for a friend's healing, use your imagination to picture your friend in the sacred host alongside you, healed and happy. Your friend is truly living along with you in the Body of Christ. Perhaps you can visualize with you in the host the others who care for your friend—physicians, nurses, family members, and so on. Ask each of them to bless and heal your suffering friend who is present among them in the Cosmic Body.

If you are having a disagreement with someone or you are alienated from a certain person, use your imagination to picture that person in the host with you. You know by faith that the person is loved by Christ and is in Christ. Speak to that person as you picture both of you living in Christ, and let the other person speak back to you.

Seeing a Relationship in the Host. If you are married or enjoy a close friendship with another, you may picture you and your partner *as a relationship* in the host, since your relationship also lives in the Body of Christ. In Christ, each relationship is a new being—a new "self"—living in Christ.

As the Scripture has it, marriage partners "become one flesh," that is, a new being. When individuals form a true relationship, they give birth to a "third being," or "third self." This third self has a life and purpose of its own. In a close relationship there are three selves—you, your partner, and the relationship. *The relationship is the "third self."* In marriage or a close friendship, the individuality of the partners is not lost in the relationship; rather, each person becomes more well–defined because of it.

Recently, my wife and I were seated side by side in a pew during eucharistic adoration. In imagination, I began picturing the two of us together in the host looking back at us in the pew. Not only did my wife and I individually live in Christ, but our relationship—who we are as a partnership—also lives in Christ. It was as though our relationship was a third being in the host. All three selves—my wife, our relationship, and I—had work to do, separately and together, in helping build the kingdom of God on Earth. I discovered that our relationship, the "third self," had some suggestions for me on how to improve our relationship.

Partners can picture themselves in the host *as a relationship.* For example, if your marriage happens to be in trouble, you may picture your relationship in the host and ask it (the third self) to give you advice or courage to keep this third self alive and well–functioning.

In the Eucharist, you can see Jesus in his human life. You can also see yourself and a relationship. But there is far more waiting to be revealed.

CONTEMPLATIVE EXERCISE 4
Seeing Others in the Eucharist

The process that makes us whole begins in each of us when we realize God's purpose for creating human life: it is for each of us and all of us to be one with God and one with each other in loving union forever.

Because the Cosmic Christ creates a divine milieu that encompasses everything, Christ is able through the Eucharist to unite himself—as an embodied Person—to all humanity everywhere. His eucharistic presence reflects the entire movement of the universe—past, present, and future—toward its fulfillment in Christ. Furthermore, the Cosmic Christ is present to all persons and things, individually and collectively. This includes everything that makes up the internal and external environment in which we live—including all matter.

Even in ancient times, the Book of Wisdom stressed that God gives life and keeps things in existence because God loves everything in creation.

> The whole world before you is like a speck that tips the
>   scales,
> and like a drop of morning dew that falls on the ground.
> But you are merciful to all, for you can do all things,
> and you overlook people's sins, so that they may repent.
> For you love all things that exist,
> and detest none of the things that you have made,
> for you would not have made anything if you had hated it.
> How would anything have endured if you had not
>   willed it?
> Or how would anything not called forth by you have been
>   preserved?
> You spare all things, for they are yours, O Lord, you who
>   love the living.
> For your immortal spirit is in all things. (Wis 11:22—12:1)

As he imparts this transforming universal presence to humans, "Christ must at the same time and in the same way sanctify matter itself, and in so doing bring to it a promise of eventual transfiguration."[5]

132

Christ's concern today is to help that Body—his Body—to grow in knowledge, wisdom, compassion, faith, hope, and love. He wants to evolve the members of his Body so that each one thinks, chooses, and acts as he does. That is his focus—to bring all things to the "promise of eventual transfiguration."

In gospel language, the Cosmic Christ with the help of the Holy Spirit is filling the kingdom of God with people who are being unified in their love for God and for each other.

Looking at the Host: Seeing Others There. You are not the only person living in the Body of Christ. Everyone is there in the Eucharist. When you are praying for individuals, you can use your imagination to picture them in the host feeling love coming from Christ. When you do this, you are affirming that they are in the Body of Christ, that Christ holds them safely there, and that no one can take them from him. You may also picture you in the host greeting or embracing the individuals for whom you are praying.

Looking at the Host: Seeing Those Who Have Died. If you are grieving the loss of a loved one or just wish to reconnect with someone who has died, you may picture them in the host, since they too live in the Body of Christ—quite alive! You may join them in the host. You may ask them for a blessing, ask them for advice, remind them of your love for them, and so on.

Looking at the Host: Seeing Your Favorite Saints There. All the saints live forever in the Body of Christ. This includes Mary, the apostles, the martyrs, all the holy men and women who have lived on Earth through the centuries.

If you have a devotion to certain saints, you may picture them in the sacred host, for this is where they live. They are present in the host and cup, just as you and I are, as members of Christ's Cosmic Body. There you may also join them, greet them, or speak to them. On a saint's feast day, you may picture that saint in the host or chalice—and join them there.

Connecting with Forgotten Others. In Christ, you become part of something much greater than yourself. In Christ, you become one with all humanity. So, using your compassionate imagination, you can picture yourself in the host and, while there, bring into your heart

- Someone who is lonely
- Someone who is grieving

133

- Someone who is depressed or discouraged
- Someone who has been rejected

Take them into your heart and bless them. And promise the Lord that, when you see someone today who is lonely or grieving or discouraged or rejected, you will say a kind word or do a kind deed.

CONTEMPLATIVE EXERCISE 5
Holy Communion Time

Joyful at Communion Time. At communion time, listen to the words of the priest as he raises the host and says, "Happy are those who are called to his supper."

Notice the word *happy*. Happy is the opposite of grim and gloomy. Let yourself feel happy, blessed, and at peace. Holy communion is a time for joy and smiles. Anyone who understands the meaning of holy communion will be joyful and smiling—and peaceful—walking forward to receive holy communion.

Notice the words *supper* and *happy* linked together. I have often reminded Eucharistic Ministers that the Eucharist is like a banquet. As waiters at this happy occasion, they are privileged to manifest the joy of a celebratory meal by smiling at each person coming to receive their portion of the divine food and drink.

In Front of and Behind Me. Each one of the people standing in front of you and behind you in the communion line is a part of the Christ that you receive, just as you are a part of the Christ they receive. So, when you take the Eucharist into you, in your imagination you may picture also taking into your heart all those people lined up in front of you and behind you waiting for communion. Imagine some of their joys and some of their sorrows and pain, and ask God to bless them.

Lift Up Your Eyes. I remember once after communion, when a priest looked out on his congregation, he could see that most of them had their heads buried in their hands in private prayer. He said to them, "Please take your head out of your hands and look up and see the Body of Christ in the people all around you. With a smile and with your love, bless them. They are a part of you because they are a part of Christ. Christ wants you to love him by loving each other."

Watching Others Receive Communion. If you don't know what to do, while you are in your pew waiting to enter the communion line or when you come back to your pew after receiving holy communion, *watch with joy as each person receives holy communion.* As they pass by you on their way back to their place, visualize the light of Christ in their hearts.

The Light of Christ. Use your spiritual imagination to watch Christ come alive within each person as they put the host on their tongue. Or picture the host as a bright light that lights up inside each person as it touches their tongue, making them glow. If you look at those receiving the precious blood, in your imagination, watch the Christ blood enter their mouth, flow down their throat, and permeate their whole being.

Connected by Golden Threads. After you have received holy communion, use your spiritual imagination to *see each person connected to you, perhaps by rays of Christ's love.* This connection is real because, in Christ, you are living with them and they are living with you. Christ's life energy is flowing through each of you. You are not only their brother or sister in Christ, but you are connected to them as they are connected to you. Through the rays of Christ's love, send your love to them and bless them.

Christ has made us all one cosmic organic reality. We are all one being in the body and blood of Christ. Just as we all live together and inhale the same oxygen in the air around us, we are all living and breathing together in the *divine milieu.*

Take a deep breath of the heavenly atmosphere that fills the church.

CONTEMPLATIVE EXERCISE 6
Habitual Communion with Christ

For Teilhard, "The Christian's whole life, on earth as in heaven, can be seen as a sort of perpetual eucharistic union."[6] This union begins in baptism. As a result of receiving this sacrament, we are permanently connected to Christ. We become formal members or cells in his universal Body. Because of our baptism and organic union in his

Body, Teilhard points out, we remain perpetually in a kind of eucharistic union. Teilhard calls it a *habitual* communion.

Because we live in Christ's own Body, we can, by a conscious choice, at any moment enjoy a "spiritual connection" or communion with Christ. In fact, as Teilhard points out, practicing this habitual communion gives a fuller meaning and significance to sacramental Eucharist.

> Far from conflicting with the Eucharist or serving as a repetition of the Eucharist, this 'habitual' communion effected by sanctifying grace between Christ and the faithful gives its full significance...to sacramental reception of the sacred species.[7]

Teilhard suggests that we explain this idea of habitual communion to children who are too young to receive the liturgical eucharistic sacrament. Children that have not yet reached the age for holy communion become united with Christ by baptism. They become members of Christ before any physical contact with his sacramental body. "Long before any communion, a first and *permanent* connection through the operation of baptism is formed between the Christian and the body of Christ."[8]

Even though reception of the Eucharist during liturgy raises Christ's presence to a special degree of intimacy and importance, habitual communion can serve as a powerful continual presence, "more strongly established, even though in a less concentrated form."[9] Teilhard explains the importance of maintaining awareness of Christ's presence in this habitual way.

> If we understand the matter this way, sacramental communion ceases to be a discontinuous element in Christian life and becomes the fabric from which it is woven. It is the accentuation and the renewal of a permanent state that attaches us continually to Christ. In short, the Christian's whole life, on earth as in heaven, can be seen as a sort of perpetual eucharistic union.[10]

For Teilhard, Christ is the inescapable divine milieu in which we spend each day, enabling us to live permanently in God's love. Because we live in Christ's milieu, we can enjoy habitual communion—a sort of perpetual eucharistic union. As we move about on Earth, the divine atmosphere surrounds and permeates us. We breathe it in. We exhale it. It is our everyday milieu. We have no need to put on some artificial equipment to access this divine live–giving spirit.

In our ordinary life, we don't need an intermediary to bring us oxygen, because there is nothing between us and the atmosphere. We live in it. Similarly, Christ is the divine atmosphere in which we live and breathe the divine life. It is our everyday divine atmosphere. Teilhard points out, "Christ is not an *intermediary* separating us from God, but a *medium* uniting us to God."[11] An *intermediary* is someone who acts between us and God, thus keeps us separate from God. Nothing can ever take us out of our divine atmosphere. It is the *medium* in which we live and breathe. We live in God's milieu. That is a fundamental truth of faith. Wherever we are or whatever occupies us, we are in the divine milieu and continually available for spiritual communion.

CONTEMPLATIVE EXERCISE 7
The Risen Christ Teaching

The Gospel according to John and the three extant letters attributed to John were not written until sometime after the year 90. This is perhaps twenty or more years after the Gospels of Matthew, Mark, and Luke first appeared, and forty years after Paul's earliest letters.

Some chapters of John's Gospel cover themes that others Gospel writers never mention or discuss, such as the following:

- Jesus's dialogue with Nicodemus about being reborn (chapter 3)
- His intimate encounter with the woman at the well (chapter 3)
- His announcement of the Eucharist early in his ministry (chapter 6)
- His almost four-chapters–long Last Supper discourse (chapters 14—17)

According to some gospel accounts, after his resurrection Jesus stayed with his disciples for forty day before he departed to be with his

Father. During those days he continued to teach them about the kingdom of God. However, none of the Gospel writers tell us what went on during those days or the content of these additional teachings.

Some theologians wonder if Jesus's long discourse at the Last Supper—chapters 14 through 17—might reflect a summary of those forty days of instruction, instead of a discourse given in its entirety during the paschal meal, as John's Gospel presents it. Scholars point out that a lengthy discourse delivered after a big evening meal would not have been a good time to present powerful theological ideas to a group of men sated with food and wine—especially since the material in the discourse was so new and important.

At the Last Supper, Jesus probably knew that he would spend another forty days with his disciples. So, it is strange that he would say to them during this special supper, "I am going to the Father and you will see me no longer" (John 16:10). This departure–announcement statement would have made much more sense if he had said it to them during a teaching session shortly before his ascension.

Whether these important instructions that John relates were given at the Last Supper or after his resurrection remains an interesting question for debate. In any case, they may be helpful to us in developing spiritual practices that emphasize Christ who is and Christ who will be. For example, Jesus's teachings on the Holy Spirit[12] recorded in John's Gospel point out the central and ongoing role that the Holy Spirit plays in nurturing and developing the Body of the Christ who is.

We do nothing to earn the Holy Spirit's help. The Spirit is a permanent gift from the Father. Since the Spirit has settled down and made his home in us, our role is to become familiar with this divine guest and learn to recognize his voice, urgings, and gentle nudging. From Teilhard's perspective, the Holy Spirit's role is to teach us how to live evolutely.

The Holy Spirit is the divine person who facilitates our spiritual death and rebirth. He reminds us that we are living primarily as members of Christ's Body. It is easy to forget that we are not just humans living an individual life. We need repeatedly to be reminded that, first and foremost, we participate in a divine life. And the divine person in whom we live is bringing about the kingdom of God—with our help.

The first step in understanding the teachings of Jesus is to undergo a personal transformation that is so powerful that it is like being born again.

The *metanoia* of Jesus also involves a metamorphosis. A radical change in one's way of *thinking* (*metanoia*) involves a corresponding change in one's way of *being and acting*. It also requires that one sees oneself in a new way, as a new kind of being—*metamorphosis*.

The clearest way to describe this process is to say it feels like being reborn with a new mind and a new body (see John 3:3–10). In a secret meeting at night, Jesus tried to explain to Nicodemus about the necessity of being reborn in order to live the divine life. But Nicodemus didn't get it. Jesus explained to him how one is born first of water (a human birth)[13] and then reborn of Spirit (a spiritual rebirth). First, one is born of human parents. Then, while still living, one dies and is reborn in Christ.

Being reborn in Christ is indeed a metamorphosis since one begins living in a new body—living in Christ's cosmic–sized Body. Living in Christ is a totally new way of seeing oneself and the significance of one's choices and actions. The spiritual person realizes that he or she is no longer living merely as an individual human being on Earth, but as a cell in a much larger eternal divine Body.

The process of metamorphosis begins in each of us when we realize that the aim of human life is for each and all of us to be one with God and with one another in loving union. Jesus made this "oneness" point clear in his prayer to the Father:

> I ask not only on behalf of these, but also on behalf of those who will believe in me through their word, that they may all be one. As you, Father, are in me and I am in you, may they also be [one] in us, so that the world may believe that you have sent me. *The glory that you have given me I have given them*, so that they may be one, as we are one, I in them and you in me, that they may become completely one, so that the world may know that you have sent me and have loved them even as you have loved me. (John 17:20–23)

Before this supreme union with God can be realized through the evolutionary process, the present challenge is for all humans to work toward becoming one with each other in love. In his teaching and modeling, Jesus gave us the way to achieve this union and oneness among us.

139

The Eucharist expresses this achieving–oneness process as it is unfolding in time.

We begin by learning to live in him (as if we were him) and following his way of unconditional love. His way is a simple formula that transcends all religions. It does not require swearing allegiance to any specific theological dogmas.

As we contemplate the Eucharist, we realize that whatever exists must live in Christ. That is *everything*. Not just Christians. Not just all humans. Not just living creatures. Not just our planet Earth. But our Milky Way galaxy and all the other hundreds of billions of galaxies in the universe. We are all together living in the Christ and in the love field of the Father.

Stage Two Suggestions

CONTEMPLATIVE EXERCISE 8
God in Hiding

"We [Christians] daringly believe that God's presence was poured into a single human being [Jesus of Nazareth], so that humanity and divinity can be seen to be operating as one in him—and therefore in us!" writes Franciscan theologian Richard Rohr in his book *The Universal Christ*.[1]

Rohr then steps back and takes a much wider perspective on the incarnation. He reminds us that we believe that Christ *as the Word of God* has permeated the divine cosmic–creating process from the first moment of creation, and his vivifying presence remained there, especially on Earth. Therefore, he writes, "Instead of saying that Christ came *into* the world through Jesus, maybe it would be better to say that Jesus came *out of* an already Christ–soaked world."[2] Rohr is saying that it's as though there were two incarnations. The second incarnation—the birth of Jesus—flowed out of the first incarnation—the birth of the universe.

Rohr suggests that, perhaps, we are limiting ourselves by looking for Christ only in Jesus of Nazareth, when we live in a "Christ–soaked world." From this perspective, "the world around me is both the hiding place and the revelation of God."[3] God is hiding everywhere, looking to be found. "Ordinary matter is the hiding place for Spirit, and thus [ordinary matter is] the very Body of God."[4]

For Richard Rohr, the first incarnation of Christ happened at the moment of creation, the second at Jesus's conception in Mary's womb. For Teilhard, there has been just one continuous incarnation going on since creation, and it is still incomplete. The emergence of Jesus on Earth marks a special moment and major turning point in this continuous multibillion–year divine project. With his evolutionary eyes, Teilhard sees a universe, which has been evolving since its first moments, still evolving. Christ is still being created. God's project is still unfinished.

But God is present everywhere as if "in hiding." Teilhard writes,

> *"The world is still being created, and it is Christ who is reaching his fulfillment in it."* When I heard and understood that saying, I looked around and I saw, as though in an ecstasy, that *through all nature I was immersed in God*. The whole inextricably tangled and compressive network of material interconnections, the whole plexus of fundamental currents once again confronted me, just as it did when first my eyes opened. But now they were animated and transfigured, for their dominance, their charm, and their appeal, all beyond number or measure, appeared to me in a glow of illumination and I saw them hallowed and divinized in both their operation and their future. "God is everywhere," St. Angela of Foligno said, "God is everywhere."[5]

Teilhard sees Earth, not as a place of sin and evil, but as a loving Mother, nurturing all the creatures that live on and in her. He pictures Mother Earth holding each of us close to her bosom. Daringly, he sees Mother Earth as God's bosom:

> And in this first basic vision we begin to see how the kingdom of God and the cosmic love may be reconciled: the bosom of Mother Earth is in some way the bosom of God.[6]

However, says Teilhard, seeing our planet as the compassionate, forgiving Mother Earth is no excuse for us to remain naïve children.

We are expected to grow up and take mature responsibility for our part in the work of God's project for Earth:

> We are not, however, simply nurslings rocked and suckled by Mother Earth. Like children who have grown up, we must learn to walk by ourselves and give active help to the mother who bore us. If, then, we make up our minds to accept wholeheartedly the manifestations of the divine will registered in the laws of nature, our obedience must make us throw ourselves into positive effort, our cult of passivities must ultimately be transformed onto a passion for work.[7]

What Teilhard means by "our cult of passivities" is the way we make or invent excuses for avoiding the tasks facing us. "I'm too tired." "I have so many other things to take care of." "It's too hard." He wants us to realize that our work—bringing Christ to completion—is the most important work happening on the planet.

> We now see that what we have to do is not simply to forward a human task but, in some way, to bring Christ to completion; we must, therefore, devote ourselves with still more ardor, even in the natural domain, to the cultivation of the world.[8]

If God is in hiding, Teilhard says, God wants to be found. The idea that God is hiding seems to occur in many religions. According to an ancient Sufi teaching, God says, "I was a hidden treasure and longed to be known, and so I created the world." Another Sufi teaching says, "You and I are the mirror in which God sees himself."

WHO IS REALLY HIDING?

According to St. Paul, in an interesting twist of perception, it is we, you and I, who are ultimately in hiding from the rest of the world, because we are living in Christ. St. Paul says that we have died to our individual selves and have been reborn in Christ. We live in Christ's Universal Body as members of that Body—or its cells or atoms. To the rest of the world, those who look at us see only individual human beings walking around, yet we are hidden in Christ. According to Teilhard, we are living a hidden "cosmic life."

> To live the cosmic life is to live dominated by the conscious-ness that each of us is an atom in the body of the mystical and cosmic Christ. The person who so lives dismisses as irrelevant a host of preoccupations that absorb the interest of other people. Such a person's life is open to larger hori-zons and such a person's heart is always more receptive.[9]

Perhaps, the more we can see ourselves as living cells or atoms in the Body of the Universal Christ, the sooner we will be able to find the Christ who is hiding everywhere.

We are called to find the Cosmic Christ hiding in the Eucharist. We are called to find ourselves hiding in the Eucharist.

CONTEMPLATIVE EXERCISE 9
Renewing the Covenant

A covenant is a solemn promise that establishes a sacred kinship bond between two parties. Marriage is an example of a human cov-enant between two humans. A divine covenant is a solemn relation-ship commitment between God and his people. In a human covenant, each party agrees to fulfill certain relational responsibilities and obli-gations. In a divine covenant, God makes promises to his people and expects certain conduct from them.

In the new covenant mediated by Jesus Christ, God's promise, fulfilled by Jesus of Nazareth, is to forgive our sins and provide us with continual support of the Holy Spirit. Our human promise is to do our part to fulfill God's wish as expressed in the Lord's Prayer: "Thy king-dom come. Thy will be done on Earth."

Now that we understand the evolutionary nature of God's will for Earth's future, we also understand our evolutionary responsibilities of this sacred kinship bond. Our challenge is to see how we—each of us—can help that kingdom grow and develop. Our job, as members of the Body of Christ, is twofold.

Stage Two Suggestions

The first is to keep transforming *ourselves* to become fully mature members of Christ's body.

The second is to keep transforming *our planet* into a place where love, compassion, and peace are the dominant forces operating among people.

Teilhard gives expression to these two commitments:

> Every man, in the course of his life, must not only show himself obedient and docile. By his fidelity he must *build*— starting with the most natural territory of his own self—a work, an *opus*, into which something enters from all the elements of the earth. *He makes his own soul* throughout all his earthly days. And at the same time, he collaborates in another work, in another *opus*, which infinitely transcends, while at the same time it narrowly determines, the perspectives of his individual achievement: the completing of the world.[10]

Although the official church, on behalf of all its members, may proclaim a commitment to Christ's new covenant, it remains for each person to agree personally to that covenant and to commit to cooperating in the divine work that remains to be done on Earth.

In this spiritual exercise with Christ in the Eucharist, you may reaffirm your participation in the new covenant. Ask Christ what contribution you may make to the grand project that God has entrusted to us.

Teilhard writes,

> That [i.e., how we contribute to God's project] is, ultimately, the meaning and value of our acts. Owing to the relation between matter, soul, and Christ, we bring part of the being [the Body of Christ] which he desires back to God *in whatever we do*. With each one of our works, we labor—in individual separation, but no less really together—to…bring to Christ a little fulfillment.[11]

Some may already know what talents and resources they possess that can help further the work of building God's kingdom on Earth. They are already carrying out their tasks. Perhaps the Lord will ask such people, perhaps you, to make further contributions of your time and talents.

Here are some suggestions for a quiet time after Mass or during eucharistic adoration:

Making a List during Prayer. It is quite acceptable to take notes while you are with the Lord in prayer. Pen and paper are often helpful—even for mystics. Notes help you to remember important things. Teilhard filled scores of notebooks with insights he had during prayer times.

If you wonder how you can contribute to the divine love project for Earth, you may begin your prayer time in the presence of the Eucharist.

First, make a list of your resources.

Second, offer them, one by one, to the Christ in the Eucharist.

Third, after you offer each, wait for a signal—a gentle movement within you—from the Holy Spirit.

To each talent or resource that you now offer in covenant, the Spirit's response may signal a "Yes, right now" or "Yes, but not now" or "Always." Or, you may sense that the Spirit wishes you to develop a talent or resource to a more mature state. For example, "You need to cultivate your relationship with a certain person" or "You need to develop that skill a bit more before you are ready to use it effectively."

The following samples suggest how you might begin offering some of your talents:

- "Lord, I am good at organizing people and things.
  Where do you want to use this ability in your work?"
- "Lord, I am good at making people laugh. Where do
  you want to use this ability in your work?"
- "Lord, I am very compassionate and patient with sick
  people. Where do you want to use this ability in your work?"
- "Lord, I have strong contacts with certain powerful
  people in this community. Where do you want to use
  this ability in your work?"
- "Lord, I am good at fixing mechanical things...doing
  creative work...operating computers...running a small
  restaurant...working with numbers...cooking and
  cleaning...promoting a product...getting people to
  laugh...being a friend...working on a team...planning
  events...teaching children...caring for animals...and
  so on."

Present each of your talents and resources to Christ in the Eucharist, one by one, and quietly wait a few moments or so for the Spirit to respond.

A divine response may not come while you are in prayer. Therefore, remain attentive for a response throughout the day. God's response may come by way of a suggestion from a friend or colleague, a notice in the newspaper, a bumper sticker on the car in front of you, a phrase that strikes you on a social media site, a sentence in a piece of mail, or a comment overheard at a meeting or a party.

The next time you are with Christ in the eucharistic sacrament, you may talk about your awareness of his response to your covenant offers. During every liturgy, the official church reaffirms the covenant between God and the people.

Each member of Christ's Body commits to the covenant at their baptism and, very consciously, when they receive confirmation. Teilhard shows how we can reaffirm the covenant each day by making a commitment to help transform Earth into a place of love and peace, "as it is in heaven." Each one is invited personally to commit to this evolutionary covenant.

Partners in a human covenant, as a way of sealing their contract, usually share a meal together and drink from the same cup. When you drink from the sacred chalice at holy communion, tell the Lord that you are personally renewing your commitment to the evolutionary covenant with him.

CONTEMPLATIVE EXERCISE 10
The Cup of Wine

The wine in today's eucharistic cup or chalice is the blood flowing in Christ's Body today. It is flowing through you and through everyone else receiving it. His body and blood give everything existence and life.

For Teilhard, the wine of the Eucharist has a special twofold significance. First, it holds all the unavoidable sufferings that the Body of Christ underwent on the cross on Good Friday. Second, it also holds all the unavoidable sufferings that the members of the Body of Christ have undergone each day since then. The wine of the Eucharist today holds all the unavoidable sufferings that the universal Body of Christ is undergoing in all its members and elements today, and each day.

What are some of the unavoidable sufferings that the Body of Christ endures each day?

Central to Teilhard's spirituality are the concepts of activities and passivities.

- An activity is *something I freely choose to do.*
- A passivity is *something I must undergo*; it is something done to me.

Activities can be helpful. Some things I freely choose to do can foster *growth* in me or in others. Teilhard calls these *activities of growth*. For example, I choose to develop a new skill, or I choose to do a kind act to or for someone.

Activities can also be harmful and destructive. Some things I freely choose to do can bring about *diminishment* in me or in others. Teilhard calls these *activities of diminishment*. For example, I decide to begin taking illegal addictive drugs or I choose to spread lies about someone.

Passivities can be helpful. Some things that happen to me can foster *growth* in me. Teilhard calls these *passivities of growth*. For example, I was born into a loving family, I enjoy good health, and I have a talent for music. We cannot choose when we are born or the family into which we are born, nor the innate talents with which we are born. These are things that we must deal with. They are passivities.

Passivities can also be harmful and destructive. Some things that happen to me can bring about *diminishment* in me. Teilhard calls these *passivities of diminishment*. For example, someone may be born into an abusive family or someone may have inherited certain mental or physical disabilities.

In a startling insight, Teilhard realized that the task of spirituality and spiritual practice may be formulated quite simply. The spiritual task for each of us revolves almost completely around *how I use my energy to deal with my passivities.* This insight applies both to passivities of growth and passivities of diminishment.

How do I make choices to use my gifts and talents—my passivities of growth—to foster God's project? But just as important: How do I make choices to turn weakness, disabilities, pain, suffering, rejection, failure, loss, sickness, death, the thoughtlessness and cruelty of others, and sinful tendencies—my passivities of diminishment—into ways of serving God?

Using the concepts of activities and passivities, Teilhard places a different emphasis on the symbolic meaning of the bread and the wine offered for consecration at the liturgy. For him, the *bread* used at liturgy represents all the activities of growth he and other members of the Body of Christ perform in using their passivities of growth. These include all the effort and energy he and others expend in making a positive difference in the world.

For him, the *wine* to be consecrated represents all the energy he and other members of the Body of Christ spend enduring their passivities of diminishment. These include energy spent dealing with all the unavoidable delays, misunderstandings, confusion, mistakes, and frustrations; the anger, pride, greed, jealousy, and impatience of others; the inclement weather, mechanical breakdowns, highway accidents, unexpected crises, personal pain, and chronic suffering.

Teilhard noted that enduring passivities of diminishment and dealing with them daily consume much effort and energy—physical, emotional, and spiritual. Energies we spend enduring suffering are typically seen as a waste of energy. But Teilhard observed that Christ on the cross consciously directed the energies he spent enduring his suffering (passivities of diminishment) to help bring about the kingdom of God. As members of the Body of Christ, we can redirect the energies we spend enduring passivities of diminishment in the same way.

If the day or week ahead for you is likely to present you with many opportunities for making a positive difference in the world, you may wish to focus special attention on the sacred host. If the day or week ahead for you appears to pose many unavoidable diminishments—and you will have to spend much of your energy dealing with your own pain, care of sick others, a significant emotional loss, financial crisis, grief at the death of a loved one, and the like—you may wish to focus special attention on the sacred blood in the chalice.

Don't make the typical mistake that many make. Each day, a certain amount of your energy gets used up in dealing with the diminishments of your life. The mistake is to think that the energy spent coping with your own suffering or enduring the many unavoidable diminishments in your life is a *waste of energy*. On the contrary, it is powerful energy that can be used for positive change.

St. Paul was clear that energy spent suffering was valuable to Christ and God's project. He explains, "I am now rejoicing in my sufferings for your sake, and in my flesh I am completing what is lacking in Christ's afflictions for the sake of his body, that is, the church" (Col 1:24).

Christ's Two Purposes. Paul pointed out that the energy Christ spent in suffering on the cross had two purposes. The first purpose was *to pay the debt for our sins*; the second was *to bring about our salvation*, which means to bring humanity and all creation to the fullness of life. Notice how Paul describes the two steps:

> For if while we were enemies, [1] we were *reconciled* to God through the death of his Son, [2] much more surely, having been reconciled, will we be *saved* by his life. (Rom 5:10)

And again:

> But now that [1] you have been freed from *sin* and enslaved to God, [2] the advantage you get is *sanctification*. The end is eternal life. (Rom 6:22)

This second purpose of Christ involves a much bigger task—getting us all to learn to love more and more deeply and more inclusively.

To accomplish this second task, Christ needs us to use *all* our energy. We not only direct the energy spent in efforts to do good in the world (using our talents to make a positive difference). We can also present to Christ the energy we spend in suffering unavoidable diminishments so that he may direct that energy to bring more fullness of life to us and to others.

These are the two intentions for which Christ directed the energy he spent suffering on the cross: (1) forgiveness of sins and (2) salvation (the fullness of life) for creation.

We cannot use our human suffering to get sins forgiven; that was Christ's responsibility, and he took care of it on the cross. At the Last Supper, Jesus said, "Drink from it, all of you; for this is my blood of the covenant, which is poured out for many for the forgiveness of sins" (Matt 26:27–28). But we can use our suffering for Christ's second intention, helping bring about salvation (the fullness of life) for creation We can redirect the energy we spend dealing with unavoidable diminishments by joining our sufferings with those of Christ, as St. Paul did, to help transform the world.

Do not waste the energy you spend suffering. Redirect it to foster growth in the kingdom of God. As Teilhard puts it,

> Now the great victory of the Creator and Redeemer, in the Christian vision, is to have transformed what is in itself a universal power of diminishment and extinction into an essentially life giving factor.[12]

Christ also uses our unavoidable suffering to transform us individually.

> God has already transfigured our sufferings by making them serve our conscious fulfillment. In his hands the forces of diminishment have perceptibly become the tool that cuts, carves, and polishes within us the stone which is destined to occupy a definite place in the heavenly Jerusalem.[13]

Teilhard sums up the influence of passivities of growth and passivities of diminishment in a prayer. He acknowledges that it is Christ's fire of love that has shaped his life. Speaking to Christ in prayer, he says,

> In a true sense the arms and the heart which you open to me are nothing less than all the united powers of the world which—penetrated and permeated to their depths by your will, your tastes, and your temperament—converge upon my being to form it, nourish it, and bear it along towards the center of your fire. In the Host it is *my life* that you are offering me, O Jesus.[14]

When you are handed the sacred host at communion time, Christ is presenting you with *your life*. Will you accept who you are as Christ sees you in the host?

Teilhard answers Christ in the Eucharist for us:

> The Eucharist must invade my life. My life must become, as a result of the sacrament, an unlimited and endless contact with you—that life which seemed, a few moments ago, like a baptism with you in the waters of the world, now reveals itself to me as communion with you through the world. It is

151

the sacrament of life. *The sacrament of my life* — of my life received, of my life lived, of my life surrendered.[15]

CONTEMPLATIVE EXERCISE 11

The Eucharist and Fire

Among Teilhard's many images of Christ, some are cosmic, and others are local, some are fiery and others are gentle, but they are always personal.[16] He had a special preference for Jesus's references to fire. For instance,

> I came to bring fire to the earth, and how I wish it were already kindled! I have a baptism with which to be baptized, and what stress I am under until it is completed! (Luke 12:49–50)

For Teilhard, one of the strongest images for Christ is of *Fire*. Christ is a Fire that can penetrate but does not destroy,[17] a flame that can insinuate itself everywhere,[18] a flame that lights up the whole world from within.[19] It radiates its deep brilliance from the depths of blazing matter.[20]

Near the end of his life, Teilhard explained what it meant to him to "see" Christ.

> *Throughout* my life, *by means of* my life, the world has little by little caught fire in my sight until, aflame all around me, it has become almost luminous from within....Such has been my experience in contact with the earth — the diaph-any of the Divine at the heart of the universe on fire.... Christ; his heart; a fire: capable of penetrating everywhere and, gradually, spreading everywhere.[21]

If we could look through Teilhard's eyes, we would see in the Eucharist the heart of Christ like "a fire: capable of penetrating everywhere and, gradually, spreading everywhere."

What if, when the priest consecrated the bread and lifted up the host, we could see the Fire of God's love bursting forth from above the altar with flames coming out of the host? How much more focused on the miracle of the Eucharist we would be!

Teilhard would encourage you to use your imagination to picture the consecrated host bursting into flame, a flame that does not harm anyone but rather attracts you, then heals and transforms you. What if, when you took the host on your tongue, it felt like being touched with a live coal like the one that transformed Isaiah into a prophet (Isa 6:5–7)?

What if, when you drank from the chalice, you were filled with a sweetly burning and transforming liquid, and you could feel that living energy of Christ flowing down your throat and lighting up your entire body? This would be a new way of experiencing the Eucharist. Use your imagination to see what it would feel like to consume a eucharistic Fire.

Scriptural image of fire to represent divinity can be found in many ancient writings. Here are a few examples:

> There the angel of the LORD appeared to him in a flame of fire out of a bush; [Moses] looked, and the bush was blazing, yet it was not consumed. Then Moses said, "I must turn aside and look at this great sight, and see why the bush is not burned up." When the LORD saw that he had turned aside to see, God called to him out of the bush, "Moses! Moses!" And he said, "Here I am." (Exod 3:2–4)

> Mount Sinai was wrapped in smoke, because the LORD had descended upon it in fire; the smoke went up like the smoke of a kiln, while the whole mountain shook violently. (Exod 19:18)

> Now the appearance of the glory of the LORD was like a devouring fire on the top of the mountain in the sight of the people of Israel. (Exod 24:17)

> And you said, "Look, the LORD our God has shown us his glory and greatness, and we have heard his voice out of the fire. Today we have seen that God may speak to someone and the person may still live." (Deut 5:24)

> And I said: "Woe is me! I am lost, for I am a man of unclean lips, and I live among a people of unclean lips; yet my eyes have seen the King, the LORD of hosts!"

Then one of the seraphs flew to me, holding a live coal that had been taken from the [fiery] altar with a pair of tongs. The seraph touched my mouth with it and said: "Now that this has touched your lips, your guilt has departed and your sin is blotted out." (Isa 6:5–7)

Fire is an image common also in the New Testament. For example:

I baptize you with water for repentance, but one who is more powerful than I is coming after me; I am not worthy to carry his sandals. He will baptize you with the Holy Spirit and fire. His winnowing fork is in his hand, and he will clear his threshing floor and will gather his wheat into the granary; but the chaff he will burn with unquenchable fire. (Matt 3:11–12)

When his disciples James and John saw it, they said, "Lord, do you want us to command fire to come down from heaven and consume them?" (Luke 9:54)

Divided tongues, as of fire, appeared among them, and a tongue rested on each of them. All of them were filled with the Holy Spirit and began to speak in other languages, as the Spirit gave them ability. (Acts 2:3–4)

…and to give relief to the afflicted as well as to us, when the Lord Jesus is revealed from heaven with his mighty angels in flaming fire. (2 Thess 1:7–8)

The work of each builder will become visible, for the Day will disclose it, because it will be revealed with fire, and the fire will test what sort of work each has done. (1 Cor 3:13)

His head and his hair were white as white wool, white as snow; his eyes were like a flame of fire. (Rev 1:14)

Some in the early church saw fire in the sacred host at liturgy: for example, St. Ephraim (306–73) said,

What I have called My Body, that it is indeed...it is sufficient to afford life to those who eat of it. Take, eat, entertain-
ing no doubt of faith, because this is My Body, and whoever
eats it in belief eats in it Fire and Spirit.[22]

Meditating on Fire. In each of these examples, it is the same
divine Fire. You may wish to meditate separately on each of the images
and quotations above. Like Ephraim, you may wish to picture the host
as a burning flame. Or with Teilhard, see the host as divine Fire giving
life to the universe.

In his Prayer to the Ever–Greater Christ, Teilhard said,

Because, Lord, by every innate impulse and through all the
hazards of my life I have been driven ceaselessly to search for
you and to set you in the heart of the universe of matter, I shall
have the joy, when death comes, of closing my eyes amidst the
splendor of a universal transparency aglow with fire....[23]

Yearning to see God ever more clearly and to love God ever more
ardently, Teilhard prays, "Let your universal Presence spring forth in a
blaze that is at once Diaphany and Fire. O ever–greater Christ!"[24]

As a simple practice using the image of fire, look around the congregation after communion and, using your imagination, see small
"tongues of fire" hovering over each individual. You may include yourself in this experience. Theologically speaking, you are merely visualizing the reality of the Holy Spirit vivifying the Body of Christ.

CONTEMPLATIVE EXERCISE 12

A Cosmic Eucharist

Omnipresence of the Divine Milieu. Once we grasp the total
pervasiveness of the Divine Milieu throughout all time and space, we
come to realize that we all live and move and have our being in this
Cosmic Christ. In fact, *in Christ lives everything that was created and
has evolved since the Big Bang.* In a word, we are all living in the Body
of Christ—the Divine Milieu. For instance, when you are outdoors at

night, you might picture each of the stars as part of Christ's hands and arms.

Teilhard prays to Christ that we too will be able to raise our vision to his universal size:

> Humanity has been sleeping—it is still sleeping—imprisoned in the narrow joys of its little closed loves. A tremendous spiritual power is slumbering in the depths of our multitude, which will manifest itself only when we have learned to break down the barriers of our egoisms and, by a fundamental recasting of our outlook, raise ourselves up to the habitual and practical vision of universal realities.[25]

Teilhard began to realize that Christ's love flows like an electrical current continually recharging and giving new life to everything everywhere. As he says,

> The Universe was by its ubiquity *potentially* becoming for me something that loved and could be loved….Love, since all time, this strange force has puzzled and fascinated the masters of human thought by its ubiquity, its fiery vigor and the infinitely variegated spectrum of the forms it assumes. But now I see that [in Christ] it is released in its pure state and so displays its astonishing power to *transform* everything and *replace* everything….
>
> A current of love is all at once released, to spread over the whole breadth and depth of the World; and this it does not as though it were some super–added warmth of fragrance, but as a fundamental essence which will metamorphose all things, assimilate and take the place of all.[26]

A New Eucharist Every Day. At liturgy, picture the bread and wine on the altar at the consecration transformed into the evolving Body of Christ that exists today. *Each day it is the same Christ on the altar, yet each day it is a new Christ.* As humans expend their efforts to make a better world, the Body of Christ is becoming more and more fully developed as well as more and more conscious of itself in all its members.

Teilhard says, "I will continue to do my scientific work so as to influence others and to live personally the transition of cosmos into Christ." You can make the same promise to God about your daily work with the commitments and the contributions you make to your family, your neighborhood, your workplace, and your church. Make a choice to live as an instrument of God's work in the world.

A Spiritual Eucharist. For a moment, realize that you, like fish in water, are swimming in the Divine Milieu and are mostly unaware of it. So, take a moment and become aware of it. *Take a breath and very consciously think of it as inhaling the life force of the Divine Milieu.* Take a breath and imagine it to be a golden light as it goes into your lungs and throughout your whole body. You are breathing in the Holy Spirit, the spirit of Christ.

Envision Love at Work Everywhere. Creative love is operating at all levels of the universe. It is a sacred reserve of energy. It is the life-blood of evolution. "Love is the primal and universal psychic energy." Like an underground river, it "runs everywhere beneath our civilization." Love is the driving force in the growth and development of human thought and creativity. "In science, business, and public affairs, people pretend not to know it, though under the surface it [love] is everywhere." Creative love is limitless.

Love—love for one another and for the whole Body—is what keeps Christ's Body growing toward the fullness of life (salvation).[27] Teilhard sees that humans who practice living in Jesus's way can explore an ever–wider range of creative love. Such explorations in creative love contribute to advances in government, education, medicine, communication, technology, and all forms of research. These are just some of the areas providing opportunities for more creative ways to show love *collaboratively.*

Collaboration in love is the true fuel or energy for nurturing growth in the Body of Christ. Such collaborative love provides a higher level of energy to empower any project that offers the possibility of fuller life for the human community and the natural world.

For Teilhard, Jesus's way fosters not only the continued evolution of the universe but also the continual development of our ability to love more comprehensively. Teilhard responds to the Cosmic Christ with a promise to collaborate:

> What can I do to gather up and answer that universal and enveloping embrace?...To the total offer that is made to me,

157

I can only answer by a total acceptance. I shall *react* to the eucharistic contact *with the entire effort of my life*—of my life today, and of my life tomorrow, of my personal life, of my life as linked to all other lives.[28]

CONTEMPLATIVE EXERCISE 13

Two Centers

When you have two realities to deal with, science advises you to keep them separate. Teilhard disagrees. He says we are to unify them, to see them as one.

For example, consider these two realities. We believe (1) that Christ lives within us individually and, at the same time, we believe (2) that each of us lives within Christ.

In deference to the scientific approach, Teilhard would have you, first, contemplate each of these realities separately to see that they are different realities. Then contemplate them as a unity and see the two as one.

Christ Lives in You. First, *Christ lives in you.* Create an image to picture Christ living in you. Here's how this reality is unique. The divine Christ is gracing your life with his presence, enabling you to be of service to God's work in the world. Nevertheless, each of us as individuals is limited in what we can do to foster the kingdom of God (or God's project). Recognize those limitations and acknowledge them.

For example, your contributions to God's work are limited by the time and place where you live—your country, your city, your culture, you skin color, your age, your family, your status, the world situation. You are limited by your physical capacities, your need to eat, sleep, earn a living, pay bills, fill out forms, attend class, report for work. You are limited by your education, your skills, your talents, your appearance, your influence, your health, your physical strength, your habits, your chronic illnesses, and many other factors.

If Christ–in–you is to accomplish things for the kingdom of God, then Christ must work within your limitations. Your abilities are finite, locked into a restricted time and place on Earth. No one is denying that Christ can accomplish many things in you and through you. Even though your work is limited, it is essential to Christ.

Teilhard summarizes,

> That is the first step. Before considering others (and in order to do so) the believer must make sure to work at his own personal sanctification—not out of egoism, but with a firm and broad understanding that the task of each one of us is to divinize the whole world in an infinitesimal and incommunicable degree.[29]

You Live in Christ. Second, focus on the other reality: *you live in Christ.* Create an image to picture you living in the Cosmic Christ, the Christ who lives today. Like a cell or atom in Christ's universal Body, see yourself moving around. For example, move into Christ's hands. Reflect on the following questions:

- What can these great Christ's hands do that your finite hands can't do?
- Where can his cosmic–sized feet take him in a moment that your finite feet could not take you in hours or days, if at all?
- What can his universal eyes, operating everywhere on the planet, see that your individual eyes cannot see?
- What can his Earth–sized ears, operating everywhere on the planet, hear that your local ears cannot?
- What can his fingers on the other side of the world touch that you cannot reach?
- What can his voice, speaking through many billions of human voices in all languages, say that your tongue and lips cannot speak?
- What kind of planetary effort can he continually expend in helping develop the kingdom of God that would exhaust you in a moment?

The Third Step. As a third step, your challenge is to unify the two realities: "Christ in you" and "you in Christ." It is a key step to accomplish, for *in faith you live both realities every moment of your life.* Each of us forms a separate, identifiable, tiny divine milieu, and at the same time each of us participates in Christ's own cosmic milieu. Teilhard explains,

It only remains for us to integrate the elemental phenomenon [our individual contributions] and see how the total
divine *milieu* is formed by the confluence of our individual
divine *milieux,* and how, in order to complete them, it reacts
in its turn upon the particular destinies which it clasps in its
embrace.[30]

As a hint for going about unifying the two images, consider each
cell in your own physical body. Are not "you" identifiable by your DNA
in each cell of your body? At the same time, is not each of your cells
enjoying its own individual life while living as part of your body? Each
tiny cell—liver cell, kidney cell, heart cell, tooth cell, eye cell—in its
individuality can do only so much since it is limited in time, place, and
ability. Yet, as a small element of your whole body, each of these tiny
cells participates in everything the "whole you" accomplishes.

Teilhard remind us of this total unity achieved in the eucharistic
consecration:

> Across the immensity of time and the disconcerting multi-
> plicity of individuals, one single operation is taking place:
> the annexation to Christ of his chosen. One single thing is
> being made: the mystical body of Christ, starting from all
> the sketchy spiritual powers scattered throughout the world.
> *This is my Body.* Nobody in the world can save us or lose
> us, despite ourselves; that is true. But it is also true that our
> salvation is not pursued or achieved except in *solidarity* with
> the justification of the whole body....In a real sense, only
> one man will be saved: Christ, the head and living summary
> of humanity....In heaven we ourselves shall contemplate
> God, but, as it were, through the eyes of Christ.[31]

CONTEMPLATIVE EXERCISE 14

Christogenesis

For Teilhard, the timeline of Christ's existence begins deep in
the past, eons before Jesus's birth in Bethlehem. In fact, Christ lives
from eternity through time, into the future, and unto eternity. For this

reason, it is very incomplete to begin a study of the life of Jesus Christ in time at his birth in Bethlehem. Mary gave birth to a baby Jesus, who was fully human and fully divine.

If Jesus is fully divine, he qualifies as God. Before his birth on Earth and even before creation of the universe, he preexisted as a member of the Holy Trinity.

If he is fully human, he qualifies as a *Homo sapiens*. He must carry within his genes evidence of the evolutionary process. This includes what the entire human race has gone through to get to this stage of consciousness and neurological complexity. Jesus's very body reflects the long evolutionary process it took — many billions of years — for evolution to produce a community of self–reflective beings.

During time you spend in eucharistic adoration, Teilhard suggests that you might reflect on the evolutionary process that allowed Jesus to have the human body that he received from his mother, Mary of Nazareth. This may not be a process that attracts you, but it may deepen your appreciation of nature's creatures, especially ones that might not occur to you to have influenced your body and the human body that Jesus took for his own.

The zoologists would say that Jesus, you, and I belong to the *species Homo sapiens*, which evolved through scores of animal species in the *kingdom* of animals. Along with all of us, Jesus's human body shared bits of DNA with fish, reptiles, amphibians, birds, monkeys, apes, and Neanderthals. It is because of those inherited parts of our DNA that we have eyes, ears, teeth, tongue, heart, lungs, a voice, legs, arms, fingers, a digestive system, a circulatory system, a nervous system, emotions, memories, and a brain. Numberless creatures, evolving over hundreds of millions of years, gradually developed the sophisticated bodily members and sensory organs that we take for granted.

You may express your gratitude to the myriad species of life, since they too live in the Universal Christ. Here are some of their contributions to your body and Jesus's body.

Through evolutionary processes, fish developed eyes and passed them on to us through evolution, so that you and I and Jesus could see the world around us. Fish also developed lungs so that you and I and Jesus could breathe.

Amphibians and reptiles developed four limbs so that you and I and Jesus could have arms and legs and move about. These early four–footed creatures also developed a basic brain that controls the body's vital functions such as digestion, heart rate, breathing, body temperature, and balance. This brain, called the reptilian brain, also manages basic feelings. And, it is the evolved part of our human brain that allows you and me and Jesus to have memories of people, places, and events.

The mammals, next in evolution, developed the three inner ear bones so that you and I and Jesus could hear. They also evolved the neocortex so that we could process and integrate what our eyes were seeing and our ears were hearing.

The earliest mammals furnished our sense of smell.

From the primates—lemurs and monkeys—we inherited the ability to develop hands and fingers that could twist bottle caps, write with a pen, tap a text message, manipulate chopsticks, and caress a child.

The hominids, which include chimpanzees and gorillas, provided for us an ability to learn, to express subtle emotions, to develop families and communities. Like it or not, we also learned anger, envy, pride, lust, gluttony, greed, and laziness from them.

Thanks to other species in the *Homo* genus—Neanderthals, Australopithecus, Desnovians, and so on, we learned to do self-reflective thinking. These almost–us peoples also endowed us with language, art and drawing, technology, agriculture, cooperative hunting, pottery, clothing, commerce, and a religious sense.

You and I and Jesus may be taking all this development for granted as we daily use our bodies, minds, and senses. But those abilities and capacities we enjoy took the evolutionary impetus hundreds of millions of years to produce.

Whether we realize it or not, you and I and Jesus are deeply beholden to all the creatures from which we inherited almost everything we dare to claim to be our own. They are sources of our anatomy, our genes, and our DNA. Within our DNA's history, we carry the stories of all these creatures and their groping to become "something more" and to bequeath that "something more" to the next generation. From them we also inherited the drive to keep evolving.

As a geologist and anthropologist, Teilhard perceives so much more when he investigates the makeup and genesis of you and me and Jesus. Once true *Homo sapiens* appeared, at least one hundred thousand years before Jesus was born, we can begin to list countless advances that Jesus inherited, benefited from, and took advantage of, such as herding, farming, baking, wine making, dining, weaving, carpentry, masonry, home construction, home furnishings, commerce, currency, banking, written languages, art, drama, poetry, musical instruments, sailing, business, industry, schools, temples, social structures, governments, laws, military, and ethical systems. These are all part of our human experience. They were part of his experience as well. He benefited from those who, long before him, gave us those advances. And he counted on their availability.

This is only a small list of necessary conditions for Jesus's appearance on Earth prepared by all those human and prehuman creatures that went before. What they gave him and us is reflected in his body and blood and in his human soul. If human evolution in all these areas of life and social structures had not been prepared before Jesus's arrival, he would have had a very difficult time getting the world to hear and grasp his message. This eons–long development also more fully accounts for the flesh and blood of Jesus that he gives us in the Eucharist. It is also the body and blood he offered to his Father on the cross.

In choosing to become a human, Christ entered the evolutionary process. In choosing to bring his message to us, he chose to enter human life as a Jew. This was a clear choice. Compared to the morality of other peoples at the time, the Jews had an evolved social and moral code with which Jesus could work, and upon which he could build. Or, as Teilhard might say, which he might evolve into his morality of love.

Jesus had come to Earth to accomplish God's work. To do so, Jesus had to evolve the Jewish social and moral code in such a way that God's work on Earth could be furthered.

This multimillion–year process that gave birth to humanity is all part of what Teilhard calls *Christogenesis*, the beginning and becoming of the Christ.[32]

In his book *The Human Phenomenon*, Teilhard traces the beginning and becoming of *Homo sapiens*. He called that process *anthropogenesis*. Teilhard also traced the evolutionary history—the beginning and becoming—of the created universe and called it *cosmogenesis*. He also traced the beginning and becoming of the planet Earth and called it *geogenesis*.

Teilhard asks us to consider the deepest origins of *Christogenesis*. Many theologians are content to say that Jesus was born of Mary by the power of the Holy Spirit. They are like the biologists who study living

163

creatures only when they first physically appeared on the planet. There is a big difference between a creature's birth and its beginnings.

If you think his birth is going back far enough to understand the humanity of Jesus, Teilhard wants to take us back much further and more deeply.

Going Back Much Further. More important for Teilhard is that, in choosing to become a human being, the divine being that we call the Son of God chose to be immersed in *matter*.

It is true that Matthew and Luke both trace Jesus back much further in his human lineage than his earthly nativity. Matthew traces Jesus's bloodlines back to Abraham. Luke traces Jesus back to the first human parents. In his Prologue, John begins his gospel story of Jesus by asserting that Christ, as the Word of God, existed before the creation of the cosmos. John says that all things in the cosmos were made by him and through him.

The original act of creation, according to current scientific calculations, happened almost fourteen billion Earth years ago. Planet Earth is somewhat more than four billion years old. According to science, what burst forth at the first moments of creation were not fully formed stars and planets, but merely countless subatomic particles and photons of light. All of them were exploding outward at the same moment from a single point.

But what has all this got to do with Christ? Or with us humans?

It is simply this. Our entire body and neurological systems are made up of some of those 14–billion–year–old elemental particles from the Big Bang that joined to form atoms and molecules and cells. Every human is made up of trillions of living cells, each of which is made up of nonliving molecules, compounds, and various atoms. Without hydrogen, oxygen, carbon, iron, copper, calcium, magnesium, and the organic compounds we call vitamins, we could not live and move and have our being. Without them, you and I could not even exist. Without them, neither could Jesus Christ have been born on Earth.

You and I and Jesus owe our ability to act and interact, not only to the fish that gave us eyes and lungs, or to the reptiles that gave us arms and legs, or to the monkeys that gave us moveable finger and toes. We also owe our ability to have a tangible working organism to events that happened in the earliest days and years after the Big Bang, namely, the coming together of subatomic particles, atoms, molecules, chemical compounds, megamolecules, and living cells. We owe our existence to matter, ultimately to *nonliving matter.*

But what has all this got to do with the Eucharist?

The bread and wine we bring to the eucharistic table to be consecrated are made up of atoms and molecules of nonliving matter. At the liturgy, *this nonliving matter becomes for us the body and blood of the Cosmic Christ.*

> When through the priest, Christ says, *"Hoc est enim corpus meum"*[33] ("This is my body"), the words reach out infinitely far beyond the morsel of bread over which they are pronounced: they bring the entire mystical body into being. The priestly act extends beyond the transubstantiated Host to the cosmos itself, which, century after century, is gradually being transformed by the Incarnation, itself never complete.[34]

Thus, the incarnation and the mystery of Christ must be rethought in terms of Christogenesis. To more fully understand the beginning of that process—Christ's genesis and gestation—we must begin with the nonliving matter from the Big Bang. On the other hand, when we look to the future, Christ's becoming and full development is far from complete. It will be complete only when his entire Cosmic Body is transfigured.

This is God's ongoing project—God's plan, vision, dream, experiment, or however you want to describe it. In a very real sense, what Teilhard wants us to learn to see at the liturgy each day is the host in the process of Christogenesis.

The Holy Spirit is not merely transubstantiating Jesus of Nazareth but also gradually transubstantiating the entire cosmos. "In a secondary and generalized sense, but in a true sense, the sacramental species are formed by the totality of the world, and the duration of the creation is the time needed for its consecration. *In Christo vivimus, movemur at sumus"*[35] ("In Christ we live, move, and exist"; cf. Acts 17:28).

> If this is the case, then we find ourselves (by simply following the extensions of the Eucharist) plunged once again precisely into our divine milieu. Christ—for whom and in whom we are formed, each with our own individuality and

our own vocation—Christ reveals himself in each reality around us, and shines like an ultimate determinant, like a center, one might almost say like a universal element. As our humanity assimilates the material world, and as the Host assimilates our humanity, the eucharistic transformation goes beyond and completes the transubstantiation of the bread on the altar. Step by step it irresistibly invades the universe.[36]

We are so used to looking at the sacred host and seeing just a small piece of bread. Teilhard is asking us to learn to "see" in the transubstantiation of the bread and wine on the altar the gradual transubstantiation of the universe. He wants us in prayer to consider the eons of time and numberless evolutionary processes the universe had to go through so that we today could participate in the eucharistic mystery and make the act of faith that it is Christ himself—the whole Christ—that we receive in communion.

Notes

Preface

1. Mary M. McGlone, "Living in Memory of Him," *National Catholic Reporter*, June 14, 2019, 17.

2. In its first English translation, the book was titled *The Phenomenon of Man*, trans. Bernard Wall (New York: Harper & Row, 1959). A more recent translation was retitled *The Human Phenomenon*, trans. Sarah Appleton–Weber (Portland, OR: Sussex Academic Press, 2003).

3. Teilhard, *Phenomenon of Man*, 219.

4. Several of my books treat these areas: *Teilhard de Chardin on Morality*, *Teilhard de Chardin on Love*, *The New Spiritual Exercises in the Spirit of Teilhard de Chardin*, and *Teilhard de Chardin's "The Divine Milieu" Explained*.

Part I: Introduction

1. For a readable survey of eucharistic theology, I heartily recommend Owen F. Cummings, *Eucharistic Doctors: A Theological History* (Mahwah, NJ: Paulist Press, 2005). He presents two thousand years of teachings on the Eucharist from the Eastern and Western churches. Especially interesting is his review of eucharistic teachings since the Reformation, comparing Catholic and Protestant viewpoints.

2. The fact that Paul's letters often deal with local abuses of the Eucharist underscores the fact that celebrating the Lord's Supper was a fully integrated and regular practice in the earliest Christian communities.

3. *Catechism of the Catholic Church*, no. 1374. "In the most blessed sacrament of the Eucharist "the body and blood, together with

the soul and divinity, of our Lord Jesus Christ and, therefore, *the whole Christ is truly, really, and substantially contained.*"

4. For more of Jesus's evolutionary activity, see my *Teilhard de Chardin on the Gospels: The Message of Jesus for an Evolutionary World* (Mahwah, NJ: Paulist Press, 2019).

5. Pierre Teilhard de Chardin, *The Human Phenomenon*, trans. Sarah Appleton–Weber (Portland, OR: Sussex Academic Press, 2003), 152. An almost identical statement may be found in *Science and Christ*, trans. René Hague (New York: Harper & Row, 1968), 193.

6. Pierre Teilhard de Chardin, *Phenomenon of Man*, trans. Bernard Wall (New York: Harper & Row, 1959), 219. Teilhard also develops this idea in a tightly written, short essay, "Degrees of Scientific Certainty in the Idea of Evolution," published in the *Proceedings of the International Philosophical Congress*, held in Rome in 1946. It is reprinted in *Science and Christ*, 192–96. See also T. Dobzhansky, "Nothing Makes Sense Except in the Light of Evolution," *American Biology Teacher* 35 (1973): 125–29.

7. The expression *Mystical Body of Christ* has an interesting history. It is not a scriptural term. St. Paul never used this expression. He simply referred to his communities as the Body of Christ. The Latin expression *Corpus Mysticum* (Mystical Body) first appears in the ninth century, but at that time the expression clearly and exclusively referred to Christ's eucharistic body. The consecrated host was the Mystical Body of Christ. At this same time, the body of the believers, or church body, was referred to in Latin as *corpus verum* (the true Body of Christ). However, by the time of Thomas Aquinas (1225–74), the term *mystical* to designate the Eucharist had all but disappeared. But, in the latter part of the thirteenth century, the expression *Mystical Body* began to be used to designate the church on Earth. It received official expression in Boniface VIII's 1302 bull *Unam Sanctam* (One Holy [Church]), while the Eucharist began to be referred to as *corpus verum*. The fourteenth–century hymn "*Ave verum corpus*" is clearly a eucharistic hymn. Thus, over a period of a few centuries, the application of the term *corpus verum* was reversed. And they have stayed reversed. Pope Pius XII's 1943 encyclical *Mystici Corporis* (Mystical Body of Christ) is not about the Eucharist but about the members of the church living in Christ and as Christ's Body.

8. In the last hundred years, our species, on average, has grown a few inches taller and our lifespan has almost doubled, from forty–nine to eighty years.

9. Franciscan priest Richard Rohr's *The Universal Christ: How a Forgotten Reality Can Change Everything We See, Hope For, and Believe* (New York: Convergent Books, 2019), provides a comprehensive and easy–to–read presentation of what Teilhard calls the Cosmic Christ.

10. Paul Hawken has found over a million such organizations, large and small, operating throughout the world. He describes some of them in his book *Blessed Unrest: How the Largest Movement in the World Came into Being and Why No One Saw It Coming* (New York: Viking, 2007). Arjuna Ardagh has done a similar inventory of compassionate organizations. His book is *The Translucent Revolution: How People Just Like You Are Waking Up and Changing the World* (New York: New World Library, 2005).

11. One may suggest that only the head of the Cosmic Christ is present in the Eucharist, but not his universal "Body," including all of us. Yet, the words of consecration are unequivocal. "This is my body." One can argue that, even at the Last Supper, Jesus saw himself as "one" Being with all his followers. See John 14:20, 23; 17:11, 20–21.

12. The Greek term is *cosmos*, which means the entire universe.

13. The word *saved* has traditionally been translated in a very restricted way, as redeemed from sin. A much fuller translation for *saved* would be "made whole."

Chapter 1

1. It is sad that the church fathers at the Council of Nicaea did not simply assert that God is love, or add to the Nicene Creed "God from God, Light from Light, *Love from Love*, true God from true God, begotten, not made." It would have avoided centuries of anxiety–generating and guilt–ridden spirituality.

2. Even in Hebrew Scriptures, the primary commandment is about love. The only thing God asks of us is to love: "You shall love the LORD your God with all your heart, and with all your soul, and with all your might" (Deut 6:5) and "You shall love your neighbor as yourself" (Lev 19:18). Nothing is mentioned in this commandment about God requiring fear, worship, sacrifice, etc. Just a response of love.

3. St. Paul concurs. "For freedom Christ has set us free. Stand firm, therefore, and do not submit again to a yoke of slavery" (Gal 5:1).

4. John expresses this same idea a number of ways in his first letter: "If we love one another, God lives in us, and his love is perfected in us. By this we know that we abide in him and he in us, because he has given us of his Spirit [of love]....God is love, and those who abide in love abide in God, and God abides in them" (1 John 4:12–13, 16); "All who obey his commandments abide in him, and he abides in them. And by this we know that he abides in us, by the Spirit [of love] that he has given us" (3:24).

5. I found this simple but profound expression in Andre Auger, *So Much to Ponder* (Guelph, ON: One Thousand Trees, 2018), 209.

6. "This self–disclosure of…God into physical creation was the first Incarnation (the general term for any enfleshment of spirit) long before the personal, second Incarnation that Christians believe happened with Jesus." Richard Rohr, *The Universal Christ* (New York: Convergent Books, 2019), 12.

7. Rohr, *Universal Christ*, 12. Paul said it long ago: "Ever since the creation of the world his eternal power and divine nature, invisible though they are, have been understood and seen through the things he has made" (Rom 1:20).

8. The Greek verb *eskēnōsen* (from the Greek for tent or tabernacle) is here more accurately translated as "pitched his tent among us."

9. C. S. Lewis, *Mere Christianity* (New York: HarperCollins, 2009), e-book 2, ch. 5.

10. Luke 14:7–14, 15–24; Matt 22:1–14; John 2:1–11.

11. Quoted on the frontispiece of Rohr, *Universal Christ*.

12. Pierre Teilhard de Chardin, *Science and Christ*, trans. René Hague (New York: Harper & Row, 1968), 167–71.

13. Pierre Teilhard de Chardin, *Human Energy*, trans. J. M. Cohen (New York: Harcourt Brace Jovanovich, 1969), 32.

14. John F. Haught, *Deeper than Darwin* (Cambridge, MA: Westview, 2003), 174.

15. Teilhard, *Science and Christ*, 57.

16. Tradition comes from the Latin verb *tradere*, which means to transmit, deliver, or hand over. Religious and cultural tradition describes the handing over of the core values and principles from the past to the present. In religion, the core values are expressed in the teachings of the founder and the creedal statements of a believing

community. Belief in a fixed and static universe are not among the core values of Christianity, although they are often assumed to be so "traditionally," and are implied in certain familiar and liturgical prayers. In an evolutionary universe, a fixed cosmos provides an inadequate perspective on creation and on God's work in an evolving world. In this book, the word *traditional* is sometimes used in the pejorative sense of perpetuating the inadequate perspective that we live in a static and fixed universe.

17. Pierre Teilhard de Chardin, *Christianity and Evolution* (New York: Harcourt Brace Jovanovich, 1971), 238–39. For a fuller discussion of Teilhard on evolution, see Robert L. Faricy, *Teilhard de Chardin's Theology of the Christian in the World* (New York: Sheed & Ward, 1967), 35–38.

18. Teilhard's scientific phenomenology of evolution is the principal theme in his most well–known book *The Phenomenon of Man*, trans. Bernard Wall (New York: Harper & Row, 1959), or in a more recent translation, *The Human Phenomenon*, trans. Sarah Appleton–Weber (Portland, OR: Sussex Academic Press, 2003). Teilhard wrote the original text of *Phenomenon* during his years in China, finishing it in 1940. Evolution provides the underlying theme of almost every article or essay Teilhard wrote before then and after.

19. Teilhard, *Human Phenomenon*, 152. An almost identical statement may be found in Teilhard, *Science and Christ*, 193.

20. Teilhard, *Phenomenon of Man*, 219. Teilhard also develops this idea in a tightly written, short essay, "Degrees of Scientific Certainty in the Idea of Evolution," published in the *Proceedings of the International Philosophical Congress*, held in Rome in 1946. It is reprinted in Teilhard, *Science and Christ*, 192–96. See also T. Dobzhansky, "Nothing Makes Sense Except in the Light of Evolution," *American Biology Teacher* 35 (1973): 125–29.

21. For Teilhard's evolutionary approach to ethics and morality, see my *Teilhard de Chardin on Morality: Living in an Evolving World* (Mahwah, NJ: Paulist Press, 2019).

22. See Teilhard, *Science and Christ*, 68.

23. Teilhard, *Christianity and Evolution*, 184.

24. Teilhard, *Christianity and Evolution*, 185.

25. Teilhard, *Christianity and Evolution*, 185.

26. Although Teilhard never formulated his law in these four stages, the four stages are clearly evident in his writings. See Louis

M. Savary, "Expanding Teilhard's 'Complexity–Consciousness' Law," *Teilhard Studies* 68 (Spring 2014).

27. Teilhard will come to realize that his evolutionary law is in fact a law of love, because his evolutionary law also explains the way love operates. Love in essence begins with Attraction and it leads to Connection.

28. Pierre Teilhard de Chardin, *The Future of Man*, trans. Norman Denny (New York: Harper & Row, 1964), 123.

29. Some materialists say that consciousness is just a byproduct of neurological complexity. Teilhard is saying that neurological complexity (matter) and consciousness (spirit) evolve in parallel, not as cause and effect.

30. Pierre Teilhard de Chardin, "*Forma Christi*," in *Writings in Time of War*, trans. René Hague (London: Collins, 1968), 267.

31. Bonaventure, "Sermon I for the Second Sunday of Lent," trans. Zachary Hayes, "Christ, Word of God and Exemplar of Humanity," *The Cord* 46, no. 1 (1996): 13.

32. Teilhard's most important essay on the *noosphere*, written in 1947, is "The Formation of the Noosphere" in *Future of Man*, 161–91.

33. Teilhard, *Future of Man*, 176–81.

34. Teilhard, *Future of Man*, 177.

35. John's statement arises from Genesis 1:3–4. Jesus confirms it in John 8:12. "I am the light of the world."

36. Rohr, *Universal Christ*, 13–14.

37. Cited in the blog "Richard Rohr's Daily Meditation," July 11, 2019, accessed July 27, 2020, https://cac.org/imagination-2019-07-11/.

38. Pierre Teilhard de Chardin, *Hymn of the Universe* (New York: Harper & Row, 1965), 84, 119. Pierre Teilhard de Chardin, *The Divine Milieu*, trans. Bernard Wall (New York: Harper & Row, 1960), 133–34.

39. Teilhard, *Science and Christ*, 77n.

40. Teilhard, *Future of Man*, 56–60.

Chapter 2

1. Christopher F. Mooney, *Teilhard de Chardin and the Mystery of Christ* (New York: Harper & Row, 1964), 71. Mooney presents the most comprehensive treatment available of Teilhard's theology of

the Eucharist in his chapter 3, "The Incarnation and the Eucharist," 67–103.

2. *Catechism of the Catholic Church*, no. 1374. "In the most blessed sacrament of the Eucharist the body and blood, together with the soul and divinity, of our Lord Jesus Christ and, therefore, *the whole Christ is truly, really, and substantially contained*."

3. Mooney, *Teilhard and Mystery of Christ*, 71.

4. Pierre Teilhard de Chardin, *Hymn of the Universe* (New York: Harper & Row, 1965), 132–33.

5. Pierre Teilhard de Chardin, *"Forma Christi,"* in *Writings in Time of War*, trans. René Hague (London: Collins, 1968), 268.

6. Our English translations describe John's baptism as a "baptism of repentance (for personal sin)." Jesus had no need for such a baptism. The original Greek word says that John's ritual is a "baptism of *metanoia*." Rather than express repentance for sin, *metanoia* describes a change in perspective. *Noia* means "mind," and *meta* means "higher" or "more comprehensive." Thus, by undergoing baptism, one consciously adopts a "new mind" or new way of thinking, perceiving, and behaving. Practically speaking, *metanoia* means that you no longer look at the world around you in the ordinary way, but you now see it with new eyes. Because of your *metanoia*, you now look and see God's kingdom at work all around you and in you. In his baptism by John, Jesus undergoes a *metanoia*. He sees himself no longer as a private person living a quiet life in Nazareth but is now a public proclaimer of the gospel.

7. The Catholic and Orthodox churches along with some Protestant denominations profess that in the Eucharist the whole Christ is truly present, body, blood, soul, and divinity, under the appearance of bread and wine.

8. Christian writers and theologians continued to assert that the eucharistic bread and wine were truly Jesus Christ's living body and blood, including St. Ignatius of Antioch (c. AD 110), St. Justin the Martyr (c. AD 100–165), St. Irenaeus of Lyons (c. AD 140–202), Tertullian (c. AD 155–250), Origen (c. AD 185–254), St. Clement of Alexandria (c. AD 150–216), St. Cyprian of Carthage (c. AD 200–258), and the Council of Nicaea (c. AD 325). To read the actual texts of these authors and many more, see "Fathers of the Church on the Eucharist" by Fr. Burns K. Seeley, accessed July 28, 2020, http://www.therealpresence.org/eucharst/father/fathers.htm.

9. In Pope Paul VI's encyclical on the Holy Eucharist, *Mysterium Fidei*, issued September 3, 1965, he cites many church fathers commenting on the Eucharist, who admit the difficulty of believing that the host is truly the flesh of our Lord Jesus Christ, but in faith they affirm that Jesus is not a liar but he means what he says about the Eucharist. See *Mysterium Fidei*, nos. 16–20.

10. In the first nine verses of 1 Corinthians, Paul describes the faithful as being "in Christ" or "in him" four times.

11. Richard Rohr, *The Universal Christ* (New York: Penguin/Random House, 2019), 12.

12. People who practice meditation talk about getting "centered." It means that their body, mind, and spirit have come together and share a single focus. Getting centered is not easy.

13. Pierre Teilhard de Chardin, *Science and Christ*, trans. René Hague (New York: Harper& Row, 1968), 56.

14. Pierre Teilhard de Chardin, *The Future of Man*, trans. Norman Denny (New York: Harper & Row, 1964), 119.

15. Ilia Delio, "Evolution and the Rise of the Secular God," in *From Teilhard to Omega: Co–creating an Unfinished Universe*, ed. Ilia Delio (Maryknoll, NY: Orbis Books, 2014), 49.

16. Teilhard, *Future of Man*, 119.

17. Pierre Teilhard de Chardin, *Christianity and Evolution*, trans. by René Hague (New York: Harcourt Brace Jovanovich, 1971), 182, 226, 239.

18. "So if I, your Lord and Teacher, have washed your feet, you also ought to wash one another's feet. For I have set you an example, that you also should do as I have done to you. Very truly, I tell you, servants are not greater than their master, nor are messengers greater than the one who sent them. If you know these things, you are blessed if you do them" (John 13:14–17).

19. Paul identifies himself and Timothy as *slaves* of Christ Jesus (Phil 1:1). Though most English translations say "servants," Paul's Greek word is *doulos*, or "slave." In identifying himself as a slave of Christ at the very beginning of this letter, Paul intended that the Philippians would be reminded that they too must become slaves of Christ Jesus, and that dedicated service to everyone was their role in the community. Note also that *slave* is a favorite self–designation among the apostles. James claims this title for himself in the opening verse of his epistle (Jas 1:1). The same is true for Peter (2 Pet 1:1), Jude (Jude 1:1),

and John (Rev 1:1). On top of that, Paul repeats that he is Christ's *doulos* in other letters: in Romans, 1 Corinthians, Galatians, Ephesians, Colossians, 2 Timothy, and Titus. The term is used at least forty times in the New Testament to refer to the believer. It seems clear that, at its core, the essence of the Christian life can be described in terms of *slavery* to Christ's work on Earth.

20. Teilhard, *Science and Christ*, 43–44.

21. Teilhard, *Christianity and Evolution*, 131–32.

22. Teilhard, *Future of Man*, 207.

23. Teilhard, *Future of Man*, 207–8.

24. Edward Vacek, "An Evolving Christian Morality," in Delio, *From Teilhard to Omega*, 152.

25. See John 17:13–26 for the Evangelist's description of this eucharistic principle.

26. See Teilhard, *Christianity and Evolution*, 56–75, 171–72, 184–85.

27. See Teilhard, *Science and Christianity*, 52–61. See also 1 Cor 15:25.

28. Pierre Teilhard de Chardin, *Human Energy*, trans. J. M. Cohen (New York: Harcourt Brace Jovanovich, 1969), 63.

29. Teilhard, *Human Energy*, 63. See also *Future of Man*, 124.

30. Vacek, "Evolving Christian Morality," 163. See also Pierre Teilhard de Chardin, *The Phenomenon of Man*, trans. Bernard Wall (New York: Harper & Row, 1959), 270, and *The Divine Milieu*, trans. Bernard Wall (New York: Harper & Row, 1960), 103.

31. Vacek, "Evolving Christian Morality," 163. See also Teilhard, *Divine Milieu*, 103.

32. See Teilhard, *Science and Christianity*, 40–41; *The Divine Milieu*, 92; *Human Energy*, 141–42, 162.

33. "And he has put all things under his feet and has made him the head over all things for the church, which is his body, the fullness of him who fills all in all" (Eph 1:22–23).

34. "For in him all the fullness of God was pleased to dwell" (Col 1:19) and "For in him the whole fullness of deity dwells bodily, and you have come to fullness in him, who is the head of every ruler and authority" (Col 2:9–10).

35. Teilhard, "Forma Christi," 269.

36. Pierre Teilhard de Chardin, *Heart of Matter*, trans. René Hague (New York: Harcourt, 1978), 94.

37. Teilhard, *Heart of Matter*, 94.

38. The earliest known text in which the term *transubstantia-tion* appears is a sermon of 1079 by Gilbert of Savardin, Archbishop of Tours (*Patrologia Latina* CLXXI 776). Its first appearance in a papal document was in a letter Pope Innocent III wrote to the Archbishop of Lyon, dated November 29, 1202. The term is also mentioned in the decree *Firmiter Credimus* of the Fourth Lateran Council (1215). From the thirteenth to the fifteenth centuries, the doctrine was elaborated upon by Scholastic theologians, and given an explanation using Aristotle's hylomorphic theory. Transubstantiation was incorporated into the documents of the Council of Trent (1545–63). Pope Paul VI's encyclical *Mysterium Fidei* (1965) confirmed use of the terminology of transubstantiation. However, faith in the real presence of Christ in the Eucharist has been firmly rooted in the church since its beginning.

39. We use the various public media—radio, television, news-papers, magazines, Facebook, Twitter, etc.—each day to convey to each other intangible things like humor, opinions, philosophical ideas, moral judgments, political leanings, and stories. We use physical media to convey what is otherwise incommunicable. *Media* is the plural of *medium*.

40. See Origen (185–254): "reverently exercise every care lest a particle of it fall, and lest anything of the consecrated gift perish" (*Homilies on Exodus* 13:3). And St. Ephraim (306–73): "take, eat this Bread [of life], and do not scatter the crumbs; for what I have called My Body, that it is indeed. One particle from its crumbs is able to sanctify thousands and thousands, and is sufficient to afford life to those who eat of it" (*Homilies* 4:4). Translations taken from Burns K. Seeley, "Fathers of the Church on the Eucharist," 2004, found at http://www.therealpresence.org/eucharst/father/fathers.htm. This site is the most complete source of quotes on the Eucharist.

41. St. Peter, the first leader of the church, discovered this when he visited the town of Caesarea. He could see that a group of unbaptized pagans that came to him had already received the Holy Spirit, the same Spirit that had come to the apostles on Pentecost morning. In that moment in Caesarea, he realized that it was not baptism that made someone a member of Christ's Body, but the Holy Spirit. Read the whole story of Peter's realization in Acts 10.

42. Since the year 1900, the average human lifespan has almost doubled, from forty–nine to eighty.

43. Liturgically, this focus on getting to be with God in heaven remains the objective of many of the prescribed prayers at daily Mass, and almost universally the explicit request of the designated liturgical prayers after communion.

44. Teilhard, *Christianity and Evolution*, 28, 31–34, 179; *The Divine Milieu*, 62–64, 85.

45. Teilhard, *Christianity and Evolution*, 160; *The Divine Milieu*, 64.

46. Teilhard, *Heart of Matter*, 201.

47. Teilhard, *Heart of Matter*, 199.

48. Teilhard, "*Forma Christi*," 269.

49. See Eph 1:22–23; 4:12–13; Col 1:19; 2:9–10.

50. Teilhard discusses the relationship between the Divine Milieu and the Cosmic Christ in part 3 of his *The Divine Milieu*, 112–55. For him, Divine Milieu and Cosmic Christ are simply two names to describe the same reality. Paul expresses a similar idea in Romans: "We do not live to ourselves, and we do not die to ourselves. If we live, we live to the Lord, and if we die, we die to the Lord; so then, whether we live or whether we die, we are the Lord's. For to this end Christ died and lived again, so that he might be Lord of both the dead and the living" (Rom 14:7–9).

51. Teilhard, *Science and Christ*, 169.

52. *Homilies on Corinthians* 24, 2[4], in Seeley, "Fathers of the Church on the Eucharist."

53. *Resurrection of the Dead* 8:3, in Seeley, "Fathers of the Church on the Eucharist."

54. *Instructor of Children* 1:6:42,1,3, in Seeley, "Fathers of the Church on the Eucharist."

Chapter 3

1. St. Paul also explains the Holy Spirit's role in the Eucharist and in fostering our life in the (Mystical) Body of Christ—forty years before John's Gospel is published. See 1 Cor 11–12.

2. The belief that the Holy Spirit transforms the bread and wine into the body and blood of Christ has always been taught. Among many church fathers, see, for example, St. Cyril of Jerusalem (c. 350) in *Catechetical Lectures* 23 [*Mystagogic* 5], 7, and Theodore of Mopsuestia

(c. 428) in *Catechetical Homilies* 16. Translations taken from Burns K. Seeley, "Fathers of the Church on the Eucharist," 2004, found at http://www.therealpresence.org/eucharst/father/fathers.htm.

3. For an extensive list of church writings, from the first century onward, affirming Christ's real presence in the Eucharist, see "Fathers of the Church on the Eucharist" by Fr. Burns K. Seeley.

4. St. Epiphanius of Salamis (315–403), *The Man Well–Anchored*, 57, in Seeley, "Fathers of the Church on the Eucharist."

5. Theodore of Mopsuestia (c. 428), *Commentary on Matthew* 26:26, in Seeley, "Fathers of the Church on the Eucharist."

6. *Sermon on The Lord's Prayer*, 18. Frequent communion is also affirmed in a letter St. Basil the Great (330–79) wrote to a woman he was spiritually directing, *Letter to a Patrician Lady Caesaria*, in Seeley, "Fathers of the Church on the Eucharist."

7. 1 Cor 11:25; Matt 26:27–28; Mark 14:24; Luke 22:20.

8. A list of covenant failures begins with Adam and Eve (Gen 3:16–19). Abraham broke his covenant with God in Genesis 15, but God forgave him and reestablished it.

9. In tradition, some have suggested that the new covenant is really a marriage covenant, in which Jesus is seen as the groom and the church (*ekklēsia*) as the bride, the bride of Christ. However, the *ekklēsia* is never explicitly called "the bride of Christ" in the New Testament. Paul presents it merely as an *analogy* in Ephesians. Just as husband and wife are to become "one flesh" (Gen 2:24), so Christ and *ekklēsia* are to become one flesh (Eph 5:22–33).

10. Similar statements also occur in Matt 26:29 and Luke 22:18.

11. Earlier in these pages, we listed several doctrinal statements about the Eucharist from Paul that have become part of Christian tradition.

12. See 1 Cor 2:13–16; Rom 12:2; Phil 2:5–11.

13. Pierre Teilhard de Chardin, *The Phenomenon of Man*, trans. Bernard Wall (New York: Harper & Row, 1959), 250–75.

14. See also John 1:14, 16; Luke 2:40; and Eph 1:23. Teilhard refers to Paul's *Pleroma* several times in his *Divine Milieu*, trans. Bernard Wall (New York: Harper & Row, 1960), 62, 122, 125, 143, 151. Teilhard gives a fuller description in his inimitable language on p. 122.

15. His encyclical *Laudato Si'* presents the clearest statement of this need.

16. Pierre Teilhard de Chardin, *Christianity and Evolution* (New York: Harcourt Brace Jovanovich, 1971), 73.

17. Teilhard, *Christianity and Evolution,* 73.

18. Teilhard, *Christianity and Evolution,* 73–74.

Chapter 4

1. "In the Mass, after the priest invokes the Holy Spirit…to transform the bread and wine into the body and blood of Christ, he again, invokes the Holy Spirit…that those who eat the body and blood of Christ may be 'one body, one Spirit in Christ.' He says, '*Grant that we, who are nourished by His body and blood, may be filled with his Holy Spirit, and become one body, one spirit in Christ.*' This is, in effect, a second transubstantiation: the transformation, by the power of the Holy Spirit, of those who eat the Eucharist into the one Mystical Body of Christ. This recalls Jesus' prayer to the Father during the Last Supper that His followers '*may be one, as We are one*' (John 17:11). The Eucharist unites us mystically together in Him as living sacramental realities." Brian Kranick, "One in the Eucharist," *Catholic Exchange,* April 28, 2016, https://catholicexchange.com/one-in-the-eucharist.

2. This "second transubstantiation" appears in Eucharistic Prayers III and IV.

3. Andre Auger, *So Much to Ponder* (Guelph, ON: One Thousand Trees, 2019), 59.

4. Pierre Teilhard de Chardin, *Heart of Matter*, trans. René Hague (New York: Harcourt, 1978), 52–53.

5. Some would claim that this biblical "mapping" in Genesis was given by God. However, any divine inspiration is always limited by the mindset of its human recipients. Hebrew scholars and prophetic writers living a thousand years before Jesus Christ could not be expected to grasp evolutionary concepts developed three thousand years later.

6. Teilhard's scientific treatise, *The Phenomenon of Man* (or *The Human Phenomenon* in a newer translation) studies the evolution of the cosmos in a way that gives evidence for identifying some evolutionary laws.

7. Teilhard, *Heart of Matter*, 52–53.

8. This is the theme of Teilhard's scientific book *The Phenomenon of Man* (or *The Human Phenomenon*).

9. Teilhard, *Heart of Matter*, 53.

10. Teilhard, *Heart of Matter*, 53.

11. Teilhard, *Heart of Matter*, 52.

12. St. Paul called this final achievement of the oneness of God with all creation the *Pleroma*, the fullness of all things. (See Col 1:19; 2:9.) For a fuller treatment of *Pleroma*, see Pierre Benoit, "*Plérome*," *Dictionnaire de la Bible, supplement*, fasc. 36 (Np: 1961) col. 164. Benoit writes, "Christ, both God and man, embraces in his plenitude not only God who is the source of salvation, not only humans who are saved, but also the whole environment of humanity represented by the cosmos, including the angelic powers."

Teilhard named Paul's *Pleroma* the Omega Point. His description of it is more complex: "It is the quantitative repletion and the qualitative consummation of all things: it is the mysterious Pleroma, in which the substantial *one* and the created *many* fuse without confusion in a *whole*, which without adding anything essential to God, will nevertheless be a sort of triumph and generalization of being" (*Divine Milieu*, trans. Bernard Wall [New York: Harper & Row, 1960], 122).

13. Teilhard, *Heart of Matter*, 53.

14. Teilhard, *Heart of Matter*, 53.

15. Paul's *Pleroma*, Teilhard's Omega Point, and the "completion of God's project" are three different expressions of the same reality.

16. Teilhard, *Heart of Matter*, 53.

17. Teilhard, *Heart of Matter*, 53.

18. Teilhard, *Heart of Matter*, 56.

19. Teilhard, *Heart of Matter*, 57.

20. Teilhard, *Heart of Matter*, 57–58.

21. Teilhard, *Divine Milieu*, 126.

22. Teilhard, *Christianity and Evolution* (New York: Harcourt Brace Jovanovich, 1971), 73.

Chapter 5

1. If you want to read Teilhard's complete text for the Mass on the World, it is included in the publication called *Hymn of the Universe* (New York: Harper & Row, 1965). If you want to read it immedi-

ately, just Google "Teilhard's Mass on the World" on your computer. One of the first entries listed provides you with a complete text.

2. All quotations in this chapter are from the Mass on the World.

3. Teilhard chose the word *passivities*, based on the fundamental meaning of the Latin *passio* as suffering, bearing, or enduring—undergoing something that I did not choose.

4. Even in eucharistic liturgies celebrated in churches today, the offertory gifts of bread and wine carried up to the altar by laypeople symbolize the congregation itself. The gifts of self–representation that the congregation brings to the altar will be consecrated by the priest and become the body and blood of Christ.

Chapter 6

1. Pierre Teilhard de Chardin, *The Heart of Matter*, trans. René Hague (New York: Harcourt, 1978), 43.

2. In the Roman Catholic tradition, the Sacred Heart has been closely associated with acts of reparation to Jesus Christ. In his encyclical *Miserentissimus Redemptor* (1928), Pope Pius XI stated, "The spirit of expiation or reparation has always had the first and foremost place in the worship given to the Most Sacred Heart of Jesus."

3. Teilhard, *Heart of Matter*, 131. See also Robert Speaight, *The Life of Teilhard de Chardin* (London: Collins, 1968), 128.

4. Teilhard, *Heart of Matter*, 44.

5. His encyclical *Laudato Si': On Care for Our Common Home*, 2015.

6. Teilhard, *Heart of Matter*, 42.

7. Athanasius, *De Incarnatione Verbi*, 45, quoted in Richard Rohr, *The Universal Christ: How a Forgotten Reality Can Change Everything We See, Hope For, and Believe* (New York: Convergent Books, 2019), 27.

8. Speaight, *Life of Teilhard*, 79.

9. Speaight, *Life of Teilhard*, 79.

10. Teilhard, *Heart of Matter*, 44.

11. Einstein described a similar expanding visionary experience, which led to his famous equation tying together matter and energy: $E = mc^2$, where E stands for energy and m for matter. The constant c stands for the speed of light.

12. Teilhard, *Heart of Matter*, 44.

13. Teilhard, *Heart of Matter*, 45.

14. Pierre Teilhard de Chardin, *The Divine Milieu*, trans. Bernard Wall (New York: Harper & Row, 1960), 112.

15. I am indebted to David Richo's blog on the Sacred Heart for many of the ideas in this section. See "16. Teilhard de Chardin," *Sacred Heart*, accessed August 5, 2020, https://davericho.com/sacred-heart-retreat/spiritual/reading_16.html.

16. The concept of Omega as Christ Up Ahead was developed in chapter 4 by contrasting *Christ who was* with *Christ who is* and the *Christ who will be*.

17. Teilhard, *The Phenomenon of Man*, 294.

18. Teilhard, *Divine Milieu*, 137.

19. Teilhard, *Divine Milieu*, 137.

20. Here Teilhard is probably referring to the Nicene Creed recited during each Sunday liturgy, by which the congregation gives assent to a rationally derived set of doctrines and principles.

21. Teilhard, *Heart of Matter*, 35.

22. Teilhard, *Heart of Matter*, 47.

Part II: Introduction

1. Henri de Lubac, *Teilhard de Chardin, the Man and His Meaning*, trans. René Hague (New York: Harper & Row, 1965), 56.

2. Pierre Teilhard de Chardin, *Christianity and Evolution*, trans. René Hague (New York: Harper & Row, 1969), 73–74.

3. Pierre Teilhard de Chardin, *The Divine Milieu*, trans. Bernard Wall (New York: Harper & Row, 1960), 46.

4. Teilhard, *Divine Milieu*, 47.

5. In English translations of the New Testament, *metanoia* is often inadequately translated as "repent." Being sorry for our sins does not automatically enable us to perceive the kingdom of God at work all around us. "New eyes" are necessary.

6. The Gospel of Thomas, logion 22. A *logion* is a saying or parable presumably of divine origin. In John's Gospel, Jesus is the Word

(*Logos*) of God. Thomas's gospel contains almost 150 logia of Jesus, at least 50 of which are not found in the canonical Gospels.

7. Pierre Teilhard de Chardin, *The Phenomenon of Man*, trans. Bernard Wall (New York: Harper & Row, 1959), 3.

8. Pierre Teilhard de Chardin, *Christianity and Evolution* (New York: Harcourt Brace Jovanovich, 1971), 16–17.

9. Carl McColman, *Christian Mystics: 108 Seers, Saints, and Sages* (Charlottesville, VA: Hampton Roads Publishing Company, 2016), xv–xvii.

10. Cited in Richard Rohr's blog, Sunday, July 14, 2019, accessed August 6, 2020, https://cac.org/incarnational-mysticism-2019-07-14/. Rohr comments, "In the early 1960s, Karl Rahner (1904–1984), a German Jesuit who strongly influenced the Second Vatican Council, stated that if Western Christianity does not discover its mystical foundations and roots, we might as well close the church doors. I believe he was right. Without a contemplative mind, Christianity can't offer broad seeing, real alternative consciousness, or a new kind of humanity."

11. For a scholarly study of Aquinas on imagination, see Frederick Christian Bauerschmidt, "Imagination and Theology in Thomas Aquinas," *Louvain Studies* 34 (2009–2010): 169–84.

12. Janet Schaeffler, *The Guiding Power of Hope* (New London, CT: Twenty–Third Publications, 2019), 1.

13. Walter Brueggemann's *The Prophetic Imagination*, cited in Richard Rohr's daily blog, Thursday, July 11, 2019, accessed August 6, 2020, https://cac.org/imagination-2019-07-11/.

14. Aquinas, *Expositio super librum Boethii De trinitate*, 6.2

15. Teilhard, *Christianity and Evolution*, 19.

16. I have no intention of demeaning the powerful value of reverential gestures and physical rituals in nourishing one's faith. For many of us, basic religious rituals—genuflecting, bowing, making the sign of the cross, etc.—served as key elements in the initial stages of our faith journey. They remain reverential gestures never to be forgotten. Without the integration of the body and physical movements in religious practice, faith may be reduced to intellectual profession of doctrines and dogmas, a faith sterile and lifeless. However, reverential gestures, like imagination, are primarily ways to lead us into and keep us aware of the personal presence of the divine.

Stage One

1. See Christopher F. Mooney, *Teilhard de Chardin and the Mystery of Christ* (New York: Harper & Row, 1966), 73.

2. Pierre Teilhard de Chardin, *The Divine Milieu* (New York: Harper & Row, 1960), 117.

3. Mooney, *Teilhard de Chardin and Mystery of Christ*, 72.

4. Pierre Teilhard de Chardin, *The Heart of Matter*, trans. René Hague (New York: Harcourt, 1978), 55–56.

5. Mooney, *Teilhard de Chardin and Mystery of Christ*, 85.

6. Pierre Teilhard de Chardin, *Christianity and Evolution* (New York: Harcourt Brace Jovanovich, 1971), 18.

7. Teilhard, *Christianity and Evolution*, 17.

8. Teilhard, *Christianity and Evolution*, 18.

9. Teilhard, *Christianity and Evolution*, 18.

10. Teilhard, *Christianity and Evolution*, 18.

11. Teilhard, *Christianity and Evolution*, 20.

12. John 14:15–31; 15:26–27; 16:5–15.

13. Perhaps referring to the amniotic fluid that fills the mother's womb.

Stage Two

1. Richard Rohr, *The Universal Christ* (New York: Penguin/ Random House, 2019), 15.

2. Rohr, *Universal Christ*, 15.

3. Rohr, *Universal Christ*, 15.

4. Rohr, *Universal Christ*, 16.

5. Pierre Teilhard de Chardin, *Writings in Time of War*, trans. René Hague (London: Collins, 1968), 60.

6. Teilhard, *Writings in Time of War*, 62.

7. Teilhard, *Writings in Time of War*, 62.

8. Teilhard, *Writings in Time of War*, 62.

9. Teilhard, *Writings in Time of War*, 70.

10. Pierre Teilhard de Chardin, *The Divine Milieu*, trans. Bernard Wall (New York: Harper & Row, 1960), 60–61.

11. Teilhard, *Divine Milieu*, 62.

12. Teilhard, *Divine Milieu*, 88–89.

13. Teilhard, *Divine Milieu*, 87–88.

14. Teilhard, *Divine Milieu*, 126.

15. Teilhard, *Divine Milieu*, 126–27.

16. Teilhard, *Writings in Time of War*, 70.

17. Teilhard, *Writings in Time of War*, 45.

18. Pierre Teilhard de Chardin, *The Heart of Matter*, trans. René Hague (New York: Harcourt, 1978), 47.

19. Teilhard, *Heart of Matter*, 123.

20. Teilhard, *Divine Milieu*, 117.

21. Teilhard, *Divine Milieu*, 46n.

22. Ephraim, *Homilies* 4:4, in Seeley, "Fathers of the Church on the Eucharist."

23. Teilhard, *Heart of Matter*, 55.

24. Teilhard, *Heart of Matter*, 58.

25. Teilhard, *Divine Milieu*, 146.

26. Teilhard, *Heart of Matter*, 50–51.

27. Love for one another and for building the Body of Christ is the pervasive theme of St. Paul's 1 Corinthians.

28. Teilhard, *Divine Milieu*, 126.

29. Teilhard, *Divine Milieu*, 142.

30. Teilhard, *Divine Milieu*, 142.

31. Teilhard, *Divine Milieu*, 142–43.

32. What Teilhard calls Christogenesis, churches of the West call the process of incarnation or salvation, and the Eastern churches call divinization (*theosis*). It relates to 2 Peter 1:4: "He has given us, through these things, his precious and very great promises…[you] may become participants of the divine nature."

33. Teilhard died some years before the vernacular liturgy, so he quotes the words of consecration according to the traditional Latin liturgy.

34. See Christopher F. Mooney, *Teilhard de Chardin and the Mystery of Christ* (New York: Harper & Row, 1966), 73.

35. Teilhard, *Divine Milieu*, 126.

36. Teilhard, *Divine Milieu*, 125.

Bibliography

Ardagh, Arjuna. *The Translucent Revolution: How People Just Like You Are Waking Up and Changing the World.* New York: New World Library, 2005.

Auger, André. *So Much to Ponder.* Guelph, ON: One Thousand Trees, 2018.

Bauerschmidt, Frederick Christian. "Imagination and Theology in Thomas Aquinas." *Louvain Studies* 34 (2009–2010).

Benoit, Pierre. "Plérome." In *Dictionnaire de la Bible, supplement,* fasc. 36 (Np, 1961) col. 164.

Brueggemann, Walter. *The Prophetic Imagination.* 2nd ed. Minneapolis: Fortress Press, 2001.

Cummings, Owen F. *Eucharistic Doctors: A Theological History.* New York: Paulist Press, 2005.

Delio, Ilia, ed. *From Teilhard to Omega: Co-creating an Unfinished Universe.* Maryknoll, NY: Orbis Books, 2014.

de Lubac, Henri. *Teilhard de Chardin: The Man and His Meaning.* Translated by René Hague. New York: Harper & Row, 1965.

Dobzhansky, T. "Nothing Makes Sense Except in the Light of Evolution." *American Biology Teacher* 35 (1973): 125–29.

Faricy, Robert L. *Teilhard de Chardin's Theology of the Christian in the World.* New York: Sheed & Ward, 1967.

Haught, John F. *Deeper Than Darwin.* Cambridge, MA: Westview, 2003.

Hawken, Paul. *Blessed Unrest: How the Largest Movement in the World Came into Being and Why No One Saw It Coming.* New York: Viking, 2007.

Kranick, Brian. "One in the Eucharist," *Catholic Exchange,* April 28, 2016. https://catholicexchange.com/one-in-the-eucharist.

McColman, Carl. *Christian Mystics: 108 Seers, Saints, and Sages.* Charlottesville, VA: Hampton Roads Publishing Company, 2016.

Mooney, Christopher F. *Teilhard de Chardin and the Mystery of Christ.* New York: Harper & Row, 1964.

Pope Francis. *Laudato Si': On Care for Our Common Home.* 2015.

Rico, David. "16. Teilhard de Chardin" (blog). https://davericho.com/ sacred-heart-retreat/spiritual/reading_16.html.

Rohr, Richard. *The Universal Christ: How a Forgotten Reality Can Change Everything We See, Hope For, and Believe.* New York: Convergent Books, 2019.

Savary, Louis M. "Expanding Teilhard's 'Complexity–Consciousness' Law." *Teilhard Studies* 68 (Spring 2014).

———. *Teilhard de Chardin on Morality: Living in an Evolving World.* New York: Paulist Press, 2019.

———. *Teilhard de Chardin on the Gospels: The Message of Jesus for an Evolutionary World.* New York: Paulist Press, 2019.

Schaeffler, Janet. *The Guiding Power of Hope.* New London, CT: Twenty–Third Publications, 2019.

Seeley, Burns K. "Fathers of the Church on the Eucharist." http://www .therealpresence.org/eucharst/father/fathers.htm.

Speaight, Robert. *The Life of Teilhard de Chardin.* London: Collins, 1968.

Teilhard de Chardin, Pierre. *Christianity and Evolution.* Translated by René Hague. New York: Harcourt Brace Jovanovich, 1971.

———. *The Divine Milieu.* Translated by Bernard Wall. New York: Harper & Row, 1960.

———. *The Future of Man.* Translated by Norman Denny. New York: Harper & Row, 1964.

———. *The Heart of Matter.* Translated by René Hague. New York: Harcourt, 1978.

———. *Human Energy.* Translated by J. M. Cohen. New York: Harcourt Brace Jovanovich, 1969.

———. *The Human Phenomenon.* Translated by Sarah Appleton– Weber, Sussex: Sussex Academic Press, 2003.

———. *Hymn of the Universe.* Translated by Gerald Vann, OP. New York: Harper & Row, 1965.

———. *The Phenomenon of Man.* Translated by Bernard Wall. New York: Harper & Row, 1959.

Bibliography

————. *Science and Christ*. Translated by René Hague. New York: Harper & Row, 1968.

————. *Writings in Time of War*. Translated by René Hague. London: Collins, 1968.

Vacek, Edward. "An Evolving Christian Morality." In *From Teilhard to Omega*, edited by Ilia Delio. Maryknoll, NY: Orbis Books, 2014.

Index

191

Index